ILLUSTRATED

Computer Concepts
Brief Edition

June Jamrich Parsons
UNIVERSITY OF THE VIRGIN ISLANDS

Dan Oja
GUILDWARE, INC.

A DIVISION OF COURSE TECHNOLOGY

ONE MAIN STREET, CAMBRIDGE, MA 02142

an International Thomson Publishing company I(T)P

CAMBRIDGE • ALBANY • BONN • BOSTON • CINCINNATI • LONDON • MADRID • MELBOURNE • MEXICO CITY
NEW YORK • PARIS • SAN FRANCISCO • SINGAPORE • TOKYO • TORONTO • WASHINGTON

Computer Concepts – Illustrated is published by CTI.

MANAGING EDITOR: **Marjorie Hunt**
SENIOR PRODUCT MANAGER: **Nicole Jones Pinard**
PRODUCTION EDITOR: **Christine Spillett**
TECHNICAL WRITER: **Rachel Biheller Bunin**
DEVELOPMENTAL EDITOR: **Pam Conrad**
CONSULTING EDITOR: **Susan Solomon**
INTERIOR DESIGNER: **Joseph Lee Design**
COVER DESIGNER: **John Gamache**

© 1996 CTI — I(T)P
A Division of International Thomson Publishing, Inc.

For more information contact:

Course Technology
One Main Street
Cambridge, MA 02142

International Thomson Publishing Europe
Berkshire House 168-173
High Holborn
London WC1V 7AA
England

Thomas Nelson Australia
102 Dodds Street
South Melbourne, 3205
Victoria, Australia

Nelson Canada
1120 Birchmount Road
Scarborough, Ontario
Canada M1K 5G4

International Thomson Editores
Campos Eliseos 385, Piso 7
Col. Polanco
11560 Mexico D.F. Mexico

International Thomson Publishing GmbH
Königswinterer Strasse 418
53277 Bonn
Germany

International Thomson Publishing Asia
211 Henderson Road
#05-10 Henderson Building
Singapore 0315

International Thomson Publishing Japan
Hirakawacho Kyowa Building, 3F
2-2-1 Hirakawacho
Chiyoda-ku, Tokyo 102
Japan

0-7600-3835-X

Printed in the United States of America

10 9 8 7 6 5 4 3 2 1

From the Illustrated Series Team

At Course Technology we believe that technology will transform the way that people teach and learn. We are very excited about bringing you, instructors and students, the most practical and affordable technology-related products available.

The Development Process

Our development process is unparalleled in the educational publishing industry. Every product we create goes through an exacting process of design, development, review, and testing.

Reviewers give us direction and insight that shape our manuscripts and bring them up to the latest standards. Every manuscript is quality tested. Students whose backgrounds match the intended audience work through every keystroke, carefully checking for clarity and pointing out errors in logic and sequence. Together with our own technical reviewers, these testers help us ensure that everything that carries our name is as error-free and easy to use as possible.

The Products

We show both *how* and *why* technology is critical to solving problems in the classroom and in whatever field you choose to teach or pursue. Our time-tested, step-by-step instructions provide unparalleled clarity. Examples and applications are chosen and crafted to motivate students.

The Illustrated Series Team

The ILLUSTRATED SERIES TEAM is committed to providing you with a quick introduction to computer skills. No other series of books will get you up to speed faster in today's changing software environment. This book will suit your needs because it was delivered quickly, efficiently, and affordably. In every aspect of business, we rely on a commitment to quality and the use of technology. Every member of the ILLUSTRATED TEAM contributes to this process. The names of all our team members are listed below.

Cynthia Anderson	Mary Therese Cozzola	Nancy Ludlow	Gregory Schultz
Chia-Ling Barker	Carol Cram	Tara O'Keefe	Ann Shaffer
Donald Barker	Kim Crowley	Harry Phillips	Roger Skilling
Laura Bergs	Linda Eriksen	Katherine Pinard	Dan Swanson
David Beskeen	Lisa Friedrichsen	Nicole Jones Pinard	Marie Swanson
Ann Marie Buconjic	Michael Halvorson	Kevin Proot	Jennifer Thompson
Rachel Bunin	Meta Hirschl	Nancy Ray	Sasha Vodnik
Joan Carey	Marjorie Hunt	Elizabeth Eisner Reding	Jan Weingarten
Patrick Carey	Steven Johnson	Neil Salkind	Janet Wilson
Pam Conrad			

Preface

WELCOME TO *COMPUTER CONCEPTS—ILLUSTRATED BRIEF EDITION*, the text that provides a fast-paced and engaging introduction to today's most cutting-edge computer concepts. This book's content along with the content in *Computer Concepts—Illustrated Standard Edition* is drawn from Course Technology's bestselling *New Perspectives on Computer Concepts, Introductory, 2nd Edition*. We've taken that impeccable content and adapted it to fit the highly visual and fast-paced approach of the Illustrated series. No other book gets your students up to speed faster! With the Brief and Standard Editions, you pick how much you want to cover. This book is just one component of an integrated learning system called CourseTools that works together to give you and your students a powerful teaching and learning experience. See the CourseTools page of this Preface for a complete description of the exciting technology-based resources that work hand-in-hand with this text.

About this Book

What makes the information in this book so easy to access and digest? It's quite simple. Each concept is presented on two facing pages, with the main points discussed on the left page and large, dramatic illustrations presented on the right. Students can learn all they need to know about a particular topic without having to turn the page! This unique design makes information extremely accessible and easy to absorb, and provides a great reference for after the course is over. The modular structure of the book also allows for great flexibility; you can cover the units in any order you choose, and skip lessons if you like.

The sample lesson shown here highlights the standard elements and features that appear in every two-page lesson.

A single concept is presented in a two-page "information display" to help students absorb information quickly and easily.

Easy-to-follow introductions to every lesson focus on a single concept to help students get the point quickly.

In More Detail discussions provide additional key information on the main concept.

Defining computers

COMPUTERS HAVE BEEN CALLED "mind tools" because they enhance our ability to perform tasks that require mental activity. Computers are adept at performing activities such as making calculations quickly, sorting large lists, and searching through vast information libraries. Humans can do all these activities, but a computer can often accomplish them much faster and more accurately. Our ability to use a computer complements our mental capabilities and makes us more productive. The key to making effective use of the computer as a tool is to know what a computer does, how it works, and how you can use it.

We can define a **computer** as a device that accepts input, processes data, stores data, and produces output. A computer is actually part of a computer system. Let's look more closely at the basic elements of a computer system.

IN MORE DETAIL

- A **computer system** includes hardware, peripheral devices, and software. Refer to Figure 1-1 for a picture of a typical computer system.

- **Hardware** includes the electric, electronic, and mechanical devices used for processing data. The computer itself is part of the computer system hardware. In addition to the computer, the term "hardware" refers to components called peripheral devices.

- **Peripheral devices** expand the computer's input, output, and storage capabilities.

- An **input device** is a peripheral device used to gather and translate input into a form that the computer can process. As a computer user you will probably use the keyboard as your main input device.

- An **output device** is a peripheral device that displays, prints, or transfers the results of processing from the computer memory. As a computer user you will probably use the monitor as your main output device.

- A computer requires a set of instructions, called **software** or a **computer program**, which tells the computer how to perform a particular task. Software sets up a computer to do a particular task by telling the computer how to interact with the user and how to process the user's data.

Why does a computer need software?

A computer without software is like a CD player without any CDs. Without software, a computer is just a device that does not let you do much more than turn it on and off. Fortunately, software is plentiful and available for an astonishing number of tasks, including software for producing resumes, software for managing a small business, software to help you study for the Graduate Record Examination, software that teaches you Spanish, software to help you plan your diet, software for composing music, and software that takes you on an adventure through a dangerous labyrinth.

4 ▶ COMPUTER CONCEPTS

News to Use boxes relate the course material to real-world situations to arm students with practical information.

Oversized illustrations in every lesson bring important concepts to life.

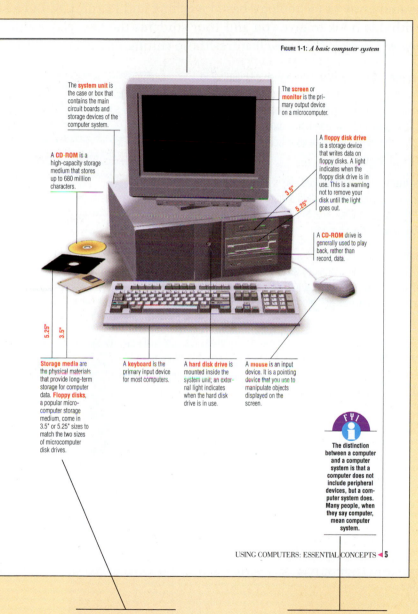

FIGURE 1-1: *A basic computer system*

The **system unit** is the case or box that contains the main circuit boards and storage devices of the computer system.

The **screen** or **monitor** is the primary output device on a microcomputer.

A **CD-ROM** is a high-capacity storage medium that stores up to 680 million characters.

A **floppy disk drive** is a storage device that writes data on floppy disks. A light indicates when the floppy disk drive is in use. This is a warning not to remove your disk until the light goes out.

3.5"

5.25"

A **CD-ROM** drive is generally used to play back, rather than record, data.

5.25"   3.5"

Storage media are the physical materials that provide long-term storage for computer data. **Floppy disks,** a popular microcomputer storage medium, come in 3.5" or 5.25" sizes to match the two sizes of microcomputer disk drives.

A **keyboard** is the primary input device for most computers.

A **hard disk drive** is mounted inside the system unit; an external light indicates when the hard disk drive is in use.

A **mouse** is an input device. It is a pointing device that you use to manipulate objects displayed on the screen.

FYI
The distinction between a computer and a computer system is that a computer does not include peripheral devices, but a computer system does. Many people, when they say computer, mean computer system.

The callouts point out key elements on each illustration and introduce key terms in red text to speed learning.

Time-saving QuickTips, Trouble comments and FYI points provide students with helpful information to round out the lesson information.

Other Features

The two-page lesson format featured in this book provides students with a powerful learning experience. Additionally, this book contains the following features:

- **Outstanding Assessment and Reinforcement**— Every unit concludes with a wide variety of assessment exercises to test your student's understanding and reinforce the material covered. Concepts Review questions check your student's knowledge of the key points in the unit. Independent Challenges provide assignments that let your students explore on their own to develop critical thinking skills.

- **Practical tips for today's computer user**—This book arms students with useful information they can apply at home or on the job. A Buyer's Guide Appendix provides real-world advice to help students purchase their own computers and software.

- **World Wide Web exposure**—To embrace the power of the information superhighway, this book provides opportunities for exploring the World Wide Web. Several Independent Challenge assignments encourage students to use the Web as a resource to get information.

CourseTools

Teaching about computers today requires much more than a great textbook. CourseTools provide you with an integrated array of technology-based teaching and learning resources that work hand-in-hand with this book to give you and your students the best classroom experience possible. *Computer Concepts Illustrated* features these cutting-edge CourseTools:

▶ **Course Online Faculty Companion**—Our new World Wide Web site dedicated to *Computer Concepts—Illustrated* offers instructors a password-protected Faculty Lounge, where you can find everything you need to prepare for class including lesson plans, graphic files for the figures in this text, additional problems, updates and revisions to the text, and links to other Web sites. See your Course Technology representative for details on accessing this site.

◀ **Course Online Student Companion**—Our second Web site is a place where students can access challenging and relevant exercises. They can find a graphical glossary of terms, an archive of templates, software, hot tips, and Web links to other sites. Students can explore these resources at **http://www.vmedia.com/cti/**

◀ **Course Test Manager**—Designed and developed by Course Technology, this cutting-edge Windows-based testing software helps instructors design and administer tests and pre-tests of the material contained in this text. This full-featured program also has an online testing component that allows students to take tests at the computer and have their exams automatically graded.

▶ **Instructor's Manual**—this book contains all the solutions to the end-of-unit assessment material, and also contains a wealth of teaching resources such as unit overviews, outlines, teaching notes, Troubleshooting tips, and Lecture Notes. It also provides four or five additional Independent Challenges per unit, as well as extensive additional resources to encourage independent study.

Computer Concepts – Illustrated Standard Edition

If you like the highly visual approach of this book but require more comprehensive coverage, then you'd probably be interested in seeing Computer Concepts — Illustrated Standard Edition. *This 200-page text covers hardware, software, multimedia, files and data storage, architecture, networks, security, the Internet and* more. *The* Standard Edition *also features 21 interactive Course Labs, which are computer-based tutorials that guide students step-by-step through different concepts. See your Course Technology sales rep for more information on* Computer Concepts — Illustrated Standard Edition.

Contents

Credits

FIGURE NO.	
1-3	a-c: Courtesy of International Business Machines Corporation; d: © Frank Pryor/Courtesy of Apple Computer, Inc.
1-4	Courtesy of International Business Machines Corporation
1-5	Courtesy of International Business Machines Corporation
1-6	© Charles Thatcher/Tony Stone Images
1-9	Courtesy of International Business Machines Corporation
2-2	Courtesy of Microsoft Corporation. Photographed by Durvin & Co.
2-6	a: Courtesy of International Business Machines Corporation; b: Courtesy of Apple Computer, Inc.

ILLUSTRATED

Computer Concepts

Brief Edition

Using Computers: Essential Concepts

Unit 1

IN THIS UNIT YOU WILL LEARN WHICH COMPUTER components are necessary for communication between humans and computers. You will also learn about user interfaces typically found on today's computer systems and ways to respond to what you see on the computer screen. The unit concludes with a discussion about manuals, reference guides, and tutorials—all of which can help you learn how to interact with a specific computer system or software package.

OBJECTIVES

Define computers

Categorize computers

Review peripheral devices

Understand pointing devices

Examine keyboards

Examine monitors

Communicate with computers: prompts, wizards, and command-line interfaces

Communicate with computers: menus and dialog boxes

Communicate with computers: graphical user interfaces

Learn to use computers

Defining computers

COMPUTERS HAVE BEEN CALLED "mind tools" because they enhance our ability to perform tasks that require mental activity. Computers are adept at performing activities such as making calculations quickly, sorting large lists, and searching through vast information libraries. Humans can do all these activities, but a computer can often accomplish them much faster and more accurately. Our ability to use a computer complements our mental capabilities and makes us more productive. The key to making effective use of the computer as a tool is to know what a computer does, how it works, and how you can use it.

We can define a **computer** as a device that accepts input, processes data, stores data, and produces output. A computer is actually part of a computer system. Let's look more closely at the basic elements of a computer system.

IN MORE DETAIL

- A **computer system** includes hardware, peripheral devices, and software. Refer to Figure 1-1 for a picture of a typical computer system.

- **Hardware** includes the electric, electronic, and mechanical devices used for processing data. The computer itself is part of the computer system hardware. In addition to the computer, the term "hardware" refers to components called peripheral devices.

- **Peripheral devices** expand the computer's input, output, and storage capabilities.

- An **input device** is a peripheral device used to gather and translate input into a form that the computer can process. As a computer user you will probably use the keyboard as your main input device.

- An **output device** is a peripheral device that displays, prints, or transfers the results of processing from the computer memory. As a computer user you will probably use the monitor as your main output device.

- A computer requires a set of instructions, called **software** or a **computer program**, which tells the computer how to perform a particular task. Software sets up a computer to do a particular task by telling the computer how to interact with the user and how to process the user's data.

Why does a computer need software?

A computer without software is like a CD player without any CDs. Without software, a computer is just a device that does not let you do much more than turn it on and off. Fortunately, software is plentiful and available for an astonishing number of tasks, including software for producing resumes, software for managing a small business, software to help you study for the Graduate Record Examination, software that teaches you Spanish, software to help you plan your diet, software for composing music, and software that takes you on an adventure through a dangerous labyrinth.

FIGURE 1-1: *A basic computer system*

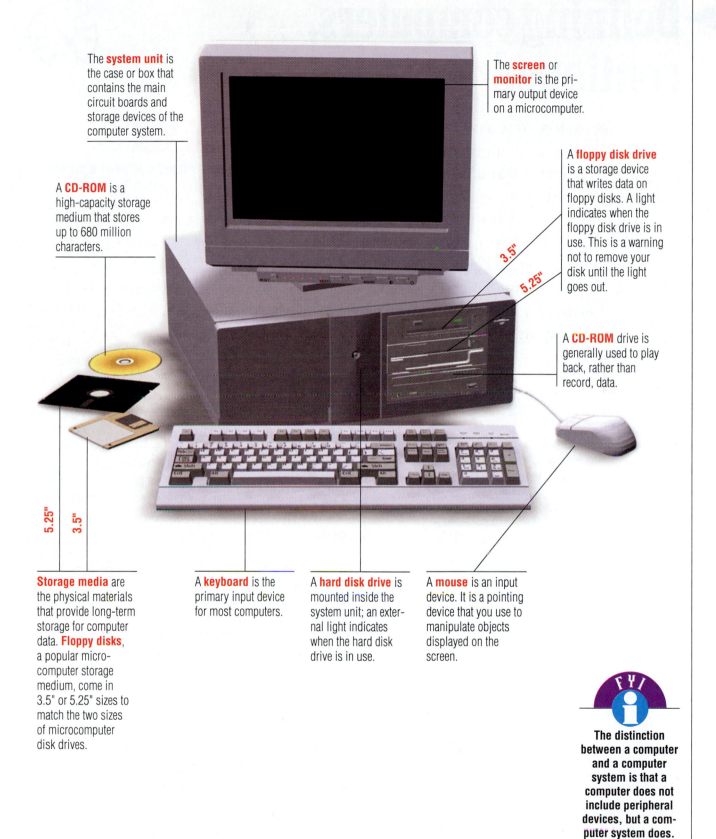

The **system unit** is the case or box that contains the main circuit boards and storage devices of the computer system.

A **CD-ROM** is a high-capacity storage medium that stores up to 680 million characters.

The **screen** or **monitor** is the primary output device on a microcomputer.

A **floppy disk drive** is a storage device that writes data on floppy disks. A light indicates when the floppy disk drive is in use. This is a warning not to remove your disk until the light goes out.

3.5"

5.25"

A **CD-ROM** drive is generally used to play back, rather than record, data.

5.25"

3.5"

Storage media are the physical materials that provide long-term storage for computer data. **Floppy disks**, a popular micro-computer storage medium, come in 3.5" or 5.25" sizes to match the two sizes of microcomputer disk drives.

A **keyboard** is the primary input device for most computers.

A **hard disk drive** is mounted inside the system unit; an external light indicates when the hard disk drive is in use.

A **mouse** is an input device. It is a pointing device that you use to manipulate objects displayed on the screen.

F Y I

The distinction between a computer and a computer system is that a computer does not include peripheral devices, but a computer system does. Many people, when they say computer, mean computer system.

Defining computers, continued

In our discussion of a basic computer system, we defined a computer as a device that accepts input, processes data, stores data, and produces output. Let's look more closely at these basic computer functions. Refer to Figure 1-2 which illustrates the fundamental computer functions and components that help the computer accomplish each function.

A computer accepts input: Computer **input** is whatever is put into a computer system. Input can be supplied by a person, by the environment, or by another computer. Some examples of the kinds of input a computer can process are the words and symbols in a document, numbers for a calculation, instructions for completing a process, pictures, audio signals from a microphone, and temperatures from a thermostat.

A computer processes data: **Data** refers to the symbols that describe people, events, things, and ideas. Computers manipulate data in many ways, and we call this manipulation "processing." In the context of computers, then, we can define a **process** as a systematic series of actions a computer uses to manipulate data. Some of the ways a computer can process data include performing calculations, sorting lists of words or numbers, modifying documents and pictures according to user instructions, and drawing graphs. A computer processes data in a device called the **Central Processing Unit** or **CPU**.

A computer stores data: A computer must store data so it is available for processing. The places a computer puts data are referred to as **storage**. Most computers have more than one location for storing data. The place where the computer stores data depends on how the data is being used. The computer puts data in one place while it is waiting to be processed and another place when it is not needed for immediate processing. **Memory** is an area that holds data waiting to be processed. Storage is the area where data can be left on a permanent basis while it is not needed for processing.

A computer produces output: Computer **output** is the result produced by a computer. Some examples of computer output include reports, documents, music, graphs, and pictures.

FIGURE 1-2: *Basic computer functions*

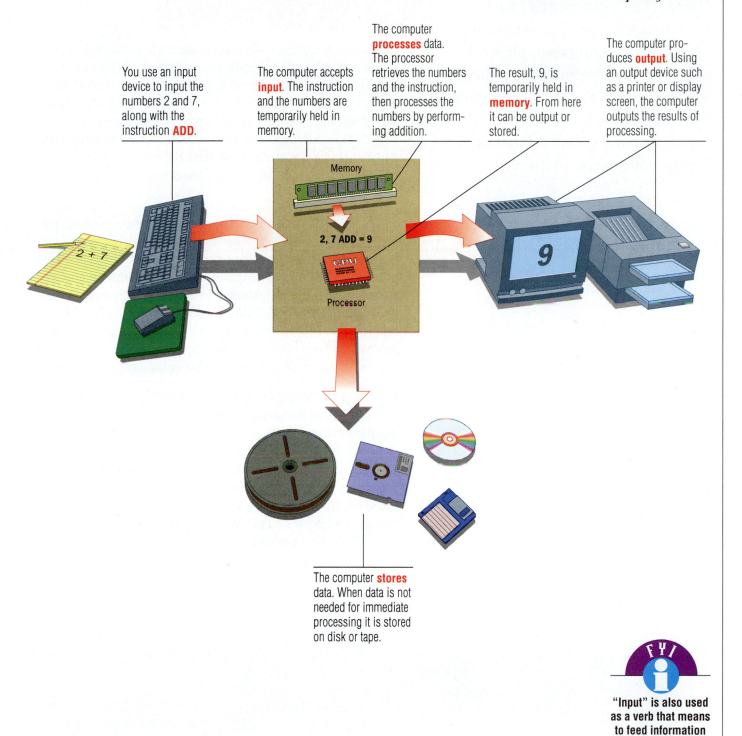

The computer **processes** data. The processor retrieves the numbers and the instruction, then processes the numbers by performing addition.

You use an input device to input the numbers 2 and 7, along with the instruction **ADD**.

The computer accepts **input**. The instruction and the numbers are temporarily held in memory.

The result, 9, is temporarily held in **memory**. From here it can be output or stored.

The computer produces **output**. Using an output device such as a printer or display screen, the computer outputs the results of processing.

Memory

2, 7 ADD = 9

CPU

Processor

The computer **stores** data. When data is not needed for immediate processing it is stored on disk or tape.

"Input" is also used as a verb that means to feed information into a computer. "Output" is also used as a verb that means producing output.

Categorizing computers

COMPUTERS TRADITIONALLY HAVE been divided into four categories based on their function, physical size, cost, and performance. The four categories are microcomputers, minicomputers, mainframes, and supercomputers. Our discussion begins with microcomputers.

IN MORE DETAIL

○━ The typical microcomputer: **Microcomputers**, also known as personal computers or PCs, are the computers you typically find in homes and small businesses. The microcomputer you use might be a stand-alone unit, or it might be connected to other computers so you can share data and software with other users. However, even when your computer is connected to others, it will generally carry out only your processing tasks. A microcomputer processor performs about 100 million operations per second. Microcomputers come in many shapes and sizes, as you can see in Figure 1-3.

○━ Microcomputer platforms: Hundreds of companies manufacture microcomputers, but there are only a small number of microcomputer designs or **platforms**. Today there are two major microcomputer platforms: IBM-compatibles and Macintosh-compatibles. **IBM-compatible computers**, also referred to as **PC-compatibles**, are based on the architecture of the first IBM microcomputer. IBM still manufactures a full line of PCs. IBM-compatible computers are manufactured by Compaq, Dell, Gateway, and hundreds of other companies. The second major microcomputer platform is based on the Macintosh computer, manufactured by Apple Computer, Inc.

○━ Microcomputer compatibility: Computers that operate in essentially the same way are said to be **compatible**. Two computers are compatible if they can communicate with each other, share the same software, share data, and use the same peripheral devices. Not all microcomputers are compatible with each other. The IBM platform and the Macintosh platform are not regarded as compatible. Both IBM and Apple are trying to overcome compatibility problems with a new platform that uses a built-in translation process to run both IBM and Macintosh software. The IBM Power PC and the Apple Power Mac are based on this new platform.

Hardware product life cycle

Microcomputers and related products are changing rapidly. Ideas for new products are everywhere; users express their needs for improved features, engineers produce more efficient designs, scholars publish new theories, and competitors announce new products. As a consumer, you should be wary of making purchasing decisions based on product announcements. A product announcement can precede the actual product by several years. Products that are announced but never made or marketed are referred to as **vaporware**.

New microcomputers and their products offer the latest features and often sell for a premium price. When a product is first introduced, the hardware manufacturer usually establishes a list price slightly higher than its previous generation of products.

FIGURE 1-3: ***Typical microcomputers***

▼A **standard desktop microcomputer** fits on a desk and runs on power from a standard electrical outlet. The display screen is usually placed on top of the horizontal "desktop" case.

▼A **microcomputer with a tower case** contains the same basic components as a standard desktop microcomputer, but the vertically oriented case is larger and allows more room for expansion. The tower unit can be placed on the floor to save desk space.

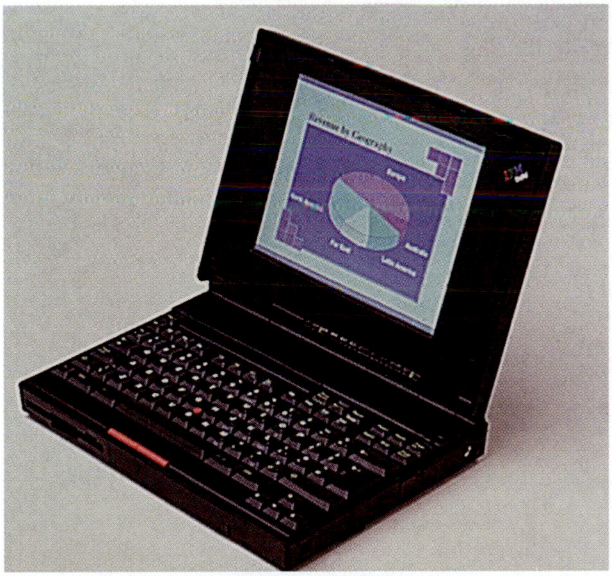

▲A **notebook computer** is small and light, giving it the advantage of portability that a standard desktop computer does not have. A notebook computer can run on power from an electrical outlet or on batteries.

▲A **personal digital assistant (PDA)** dispenses with the size and weight of a keyboard. PDAs accept input written with a special stylus.

FYI

Because about two-thirds of the microcomputers in use today are IBM-compatible, the examples in this book focus on the IBM platform.

Categorizing computers, continued

MICROCOMPUTERS ARE FAMILIAR TO us in our daily lives. However, it is important to become familiar with computers in the three other categories of computers as well: minicomputers, mainframes, and supercomputers.

IN MORE DETAIL

○━ **Minicomputers** are somewhat larger than microcomputers and are generally used in business and industry for specific tasks, such as processing payroll. One minicomputer can carry out the processing tasks for many users. If you are using a minicomputer system, you use a terminal to input your processing requests and view the results. A **terminal** is a device used for input and output, but not for processing. Your terminal transmits your processing request to the minicomputer. The minicomputer sends back results to your terminal when the processing is complete. The minicomputer system with several terminals in Figure 1-4 is fairly typical.

○━ **Mainframes** are large, fast, and fairly expensive computers, generally used by business or government to provide centralized storage, processing, and management for large amounts of data and to provide that data on demand to many users. Mainframes remain the computer of choice in situations where reliability, data security, and centralized control are necessary. As with a minicomputer, one mainframe computer carries out processing tasks for multiple users who input processing requests using a terminal. To process large amounts of data, mainframes often include more than one processing unit. One processing unit directs overall operations. A second processing unit handles communication with all the users requesting data. A third processing unit finds the data requested by users. A typical mainframe computer is shown in Figure 1-5.

○━ **Supercomputers** are the largest, fastest, and most expensive type of computer. Unlike minicomputers and mainframes, supercomputers are not designed to optimize processing for multiple users. Instead, supercomputers use their significant processing power to solve a few very difficult problems such as predicting the weather and modeling nuclear reactions. The speed of a supercomputer can reach one trillion instructions per second. A picture of a supercomputer is shown in Figure 1-6.

Computer networks

A **computer network** is a collection of computers and other devices connected to share data, hardware, and software. A network can connect microcomputers, minicomputers, and mainframes. A network has advantages for an organization and its users. For example, if a group of users shares a printer on a network, the organization saves money because it does not have to purchase a printer for every user. Network users can send messages to others on the network and retrieve data from a centralized storage device.

FIGURE 1-4: *A typical minicomputer*

► The **minicomputer** handles processing tasks for multiple users. This minicomputer can handle up to 20 users.

The **minicomputer's printer** provides printed output for all the users.

The **minicomputer's storage device** contains data for all the users in one centralized location.

Terminals act as each user's main input and output device. The terminal has a keyboard for input and a display screen for output, but it does not process the user's data. Instead, processing requests must be transmitted from the terminal to the minicomputer.

FIGURE 1-5: *An IBM mainframe computer*

Main computer has many processing units

Terminals for main input and output

Storage devices

Printer

FIGURE 1-6: *A supercomputer*

Reviewing peripheral devices

Unit 1

MICROCOMPUTER, MINICOMPUTER, mainframe, and supercomputer systems all include peripheral devices which are used to input, output, and store data. This lesson discusses the hardware components you are likely to use on a typical microcomputer system.

IN MORE DETAIL

○━ What are peripheral devices? **Peripheral devices** are equipment used with a computer. They are devices that are "outside" of, or in addition to, the computer. For example, a printer is a popular peripheral device used with microcomputers, minicomputers, and mainframe computers, but the computer can function without one. The keyboard, monitor, mouse, and disk drive for your microcomputer are also peripheral devices, even though they were included with your basic computer system. Figure 1-7 shows some of the more popular peripheral devices used with microcomputers.

○━ Why use peripheral devices? Peripheral devices allow you to expand and modify your basic computer system. For example, you might purchase a computer that includes a mouse, but you might want to modify your system by purchasing a trackball to use instead of the mouse. You might want to expand your computer's capabilities by adding a scanner so you can input photographs.

Installing peripheral devices

Most microcomputer peripheral devices are designed for installation by users who don't have technical expertise. When you buy a peripheral device it usually comes with installation instructions and specially designed software. You should carefully follow the instructions to install the device. The instructions will also give you directions on how to install any software that might be necessary to use the peripheral device. The Plug and Play feature in Windows 95 lets the system do all the installing and configuring of additional peripheral devices. Plug and Play identifies the new device and sets it up to work with your computer system.

FIGURE 1-7: *Peripheral devices*

INPUT DEVICES

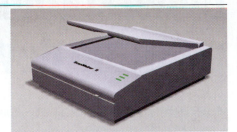

▲ A **keyboard** is the main input device for most computer systems

▶ A **mouse** is a pointing device you use to manipulate on-screen objects.

▲ A **trackball** is a pointing device that you might use as an alternative to a mouse. You roll the ball to position the pointer on the screen. Unlike a mouse, a trackball doesn't move on the desk and therefore requires less space.

▲ A **bar code reader** gathers input data by reading bar codes, such as the universal product codes on supermarket products. Bar code readers are also used at library circulation desks to track books.

▲ A **scanner** converts text or images on paper documents into an electronic format that the computer can display, print, and store.

▲ A **hand scanner** converts a 4-6" section of text or graphics into electronic format. To use the scanner, you pull it over the text you want to convert.

OUTPUT PROJECTION DEVICES

▲ A **monitor** is an output device the computer uses to display the results of processing. A touch-sensitive

screen displays options you can select by touching them on the screen.

◀ A **computer projector** generates a large image of what's on the computer screen. Suitable for conference and lecture presentations.

OUTPUT PRINTING DEVICES

▲ A **laser printer** uses the same technology as a photocopier to print professional-quality

text and graphics. Heat fuses a fine dark powder, called toner, onto paper to create text and images.

◀ An **LCD projection display panel** is placed on an overhead projector to produce a large display of the information shown on the computer screen.

▲ An **ink jet printer** is a non-impact printer that ejects ink

onto paper to create high quality characters and graphics.

▶ A **plotter** uses pens to draw an image on paper. Plotters are often used by architects and engineers to produce multicolor line drawings.

OTHER PERIPHERALS

▲ A **disk drive** stores data.

▶ A **sound card** can be installed inside the system unit to give a computer the capability to accept audio input from a microphone, play sound files stored on disks or CD-ROMs, and produce audio output

through speakers or earphones.

▶ A **modem** transfers data from one computer to another over telephone lines. An external modem has its own case. An internal modem is installed inside the computer system unit.

QUICK TIP

Always make sure the computer is turned off before you attempt to connect a peripheral device so you don't damage your computer system.

Understanding pointing devices

POINTING DEVICES SUCH AS A MOUSE, a trackball, or a lightpen help you manipulate objects and select menu options. The most popular pointing device is the mouse. Virtually every computer is equipped with a mouse. Figure 1-8 shows you how to hold and use a mouse.

Why some mice have three buttons and others have one or two

The mouse you use with a Macintosh computer only has one button. IBM-compatible computers use either a two- or three-button mouse. A two-button mouse allows you to right click an object, which provides another way of manipulating the object. For example, if clicking the left button selects an object, clicking the right button might bring up a menu of actions you can do with the object. On a three-button mouse, you rarely use the third button. Some three-button mice, however, allow you to click the middle button once instead of double-clicking the left mouse button. This feature is useful for people who have trouble double-clicking. It also helps prevent some muscular stress injuries that result from excessive clicking.

FIGURE 1-8: *Using a mouse*

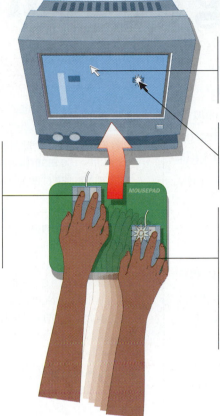

A pointer on the screen, usually shaped like an arrow, moves as you move the mouse.

To select an object, use the mouse to position the pointer on the object, then click the left mouse button.

To hold the mouse, rest the palm of your right hand on the mouse so your index finger is positioned over the left mouse button. Lightly grasp the mouse using your thumb and ring finger.

If you move the mouse to the right on your desk, the pointer moves to the right on your screen. When you pull the mouse toward the front of the desk, the pointer moves to the bottom of the screen.

QUICK TIP

If you are left handed, you can hold the mouse in your left hand and click the right mouse button. Most software has a left handed mouse option to switch the functions of the mouse buttons.

FIGURE 1-9: *Notebook pointing devices*

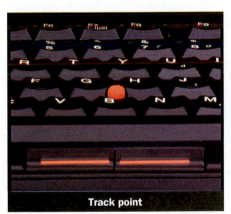

Track point

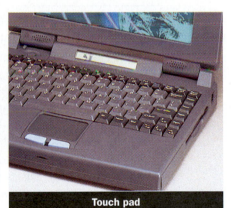

Touch pad

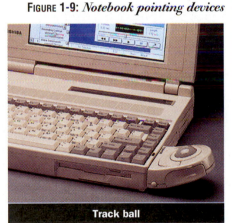

Track ball

▲ A track point is a small eraser-like device embedded among the typing keys. To control the on-screen pointer, you push the track point up, left, right, or down. Buttons for clicking and double-clicking are located in front of the spacebar.

▲ A touch pad is a touch-sensitive device. By dragging your finger over the surface, you control the on-screen pointer. Two buttons equivalent to mouse buttons are located in front of the touch pad.

▲ A track ball is like an upside-down mouse. By rolling the ball with your fingers, you control the on-screen pointer. Buttons for clicking are often located above or to the side of the track ball.

TROUBLE

Suppose you are dragging an object, but your mouse runs into an obstacle on your desk. You can just pick up the mouse, move it to a clear space, and continue dragging.

Examining keyboards

MOST COMPUTERS ARE EQUIPPED with a **keyboard** as the primary input device. A computer keyboard includes keys or buttons with letters and numbers as well as several keys with special characters and special words to control computer-specific tasks. Virtually every computer user interface requires you to use a keyboard. You don't have to be a great typist, but to use a computer effectively, you should be familiar with the computer keyboard and its special keys. Figure 1-10 shows you the location of the keys on a standard computer keyboard.

IN MORE DETAIL

☞ You use the keys to input commands, respond to prompts, and type the text of documents. A cursor or an insertion point indicates where the characters you type will appear. The **cursor** appears on the screen as a flashing underline. The **insertion point** appears on the screen as a flashing vertical bar. You can change the location of the cursor or insertion point using the arrow keys or the mouse.

☞ The **numeric keypad** provides you with a calculator-style input device for numbers and arithmetic symbols. You can type numbers using either the set of number keys at the top of the keyboard or the keys on the numeric keypad. Notice that some keys on the numeric keypad contain two symbols. When the Num Lock key is activated, the numeric keypad will produce numbers. When the Num Lock key is not activated, the keys on the numeric keypad move the cursor in the direction indicated by the arrows on the keys.

The Num Lock key is an example of a toggle key. A **toggle key** switches back and forth between two modes. The Caps Lock key is also a toggle key. When you press the Caps Lock key you switch or "toggle" into uppercase mode. When you press the Caps Lock key again you toggle back into lowercase mode.

☞ **Function keys**, those keys numbered F1 through F12, are located either at the top or along the side of your keyboard. They were added to computer keyboards to initiate commands. For example, with many software packages [F1] is the key you press to get help. The problem with function keys is that they are not standardized. In one program, you might press [F7] to save a document; but in another program, you might press [F5].

☞ **Modifier keys**: [Ctrl] (Control), [Alt], and [Shift] keys: There are 12 function keys, but you usually need more than 12 commands to control software. Therefore, you can use the [Ctrl], [Alt], and [Shift] keys in conjunction with the function keys to expand the repertory of available commands. The [Alt] and [Ctrl] modifier keys also work in conjunction with the letter keys. Instead of using the mouse, you might use the [Alt] or [Ctrl] keys in combination with letter keys to access menu options. If you see Alt+F1, [Alt F1], Alt-F1, or Alt F1 on the screen or in an instruction manual, it means to hold down the [Alt] key and press [F1], then release both keys. You might see similar notations for using the [Ctrl] or [Shift] keys.

FIGURE 1-10: *The computer keyboard*

The **Esc** or "escape" key cancels an operation.

The **function keys** execute commands, such as centering a line of text or boldfacing text. The command associated with each function key depends on the software you are using.

Each time you press the **Backspace key**, one character to the left of the cursor is deleted. If you hold down the backspace key, multiple characters to the left are deleted one by one until you release it.

The **Print Screen key** prints the contents of the screen when you use some software. With other software, the Print Screen key stores a copy of your screen in memory that you can manipulate or print with draw or paint software.

The function of the **Scroll Lock key** depends on the software you are using. This key is rarely used with today's software.

The **Num Lock key** is a toggle key that switches between number keys and cursor keys on the numeric keypad.

The **Pause key** stops the current task your computer is performing. You might need to hold down both the Ctrl key and the Pause key to stop the task.

Indicator lights show you the status of each toggle key: Num Lock, Caps Lock, and Scroll Lock. The Power light indicates whether the computer is on or off.

The **Caps Lock key** capitalizes all the letters you type when it is engaged, but does not produce the top symbol on keys that contain two symbols. This key is a **toggle key**, which means that each time you press it, you switch between uppercase and lowercase modes. There is usually an indicator light on the keyboard to show which mode you are in.

Hold down the **Ctrl key** while you press another key. The result of Ctrl key combinations depends on the software you are using.

Hold down the **Alt key** while you press another key. The result of Alt key combinations depends on the software you are using.

Press **Enter** when you finish typing a command.

Hold down the **Shift key** while you press another key. The Shift key capitalizes letters and produces the top symbol on keys that contain two symbols.

End takes you to the end of the line or the end of a document, depending on the software you are using.

The **cursor keys** move your position on the screen up, down, right, or left.

Page Up displays the previous screen of information. **Page Down** displays the next screen of information.

Home takes you to the beginning of a line or the beginning of a document, depending on the software you are using.

TROUBLE?
If you are having wrist problems and you are using a mouse and a keyboard, you may want to try using a touch pad as your input device.

FYI
[Ctrl]+[C] has been used since the early days of computing to tell the computer to stop what it is doing. [Ctrl]+[C] rarely works in today's graphical user interfaces, but the [Esc] key often cancels your last command.

Examining monitors

THE PRIMARY OUTPUT DEVICE ON A microcomputer is the monitor. A **monitor** is a display device that converts the electrical signals from the computer into points of light on a screen to form an image. A monitor is a required output device for just about every computer-user interface. Whereas you manipulate the keyboard and mouse to communicate with the computer, the monitor is what the computer manipulates to communicate with you by displaying results, prompts, menus, and graphical objects. Monitors are manufactured with different features that determine whether they can display color and graphics. See Figure 1-11 for an example of a monitor.

IN MORE DETAIL

○━ Monochrome monitors: The first microcomputer monitors and the displays on many terminals still in use today are character-based. A **character-based display** divides the screen into a grid of rectangles which can each display a single character. The set of characters that the screen can display is not modifiable; therefore, it is not possible to display different sizes or styles of characters. The only graphics possible on character-based displays are those composed of underlines, exclamation points, and other symbols that already exist in the character set.

Character-based displays use only one color to display text on a black background. Green is probably the most frequently used color, followed by amber and white. Even though there appears to be "color" on the screen of a character-based display, it is technically classified as a monochrome display.

○━ Color monitors: A **graphics display** or **bit-map display** divides the screen into a matrix of small dots called **pixels**. Any characters or graphics the computer displays on the screen must be constructed of dot patterns within the screen matrix. The more dots your screen displays in the matrix, the higher the **resolution**. A high-resolution monitor can produce complex graphical images and text that is easier to read than a low-resolution monitor. Most of the monitors on microcomputers have bit-map display capabilities. This provides the flexibility to display characters in different sizes and styles as well as graphical objects.

Monochrome or gray-scale monitors display text and graphics in shades of gray. Color monitors allow the user to create pleasing screen designs and to use color as a cue to direct the viewer's attention to important screen elements.

Printers

After monitors, printers are the second most common peripheral output device for many computer systems. This is because if you want to have a hard copy (paper copy) of your output, you need a printer. Typically, printers are sold separately from the computer system so consumers can choose the quality, features, and price they want. Ink jet and personal laser printers provide high quality print on plain paper. If you want color printouts, color ink jet printers offer the best price-performance value because of the high price of color laser printers and the poor quality of color dot matrix printers. See Figure 1-12 for an example of a laser printer.

FIGURE 1-11: *A monitor*

▶ A **monitor** is an output device the computer uses to display the results of processing.

FIGURE 1-12: *A laser printer*

▶ A **laser printer** uses the same technology as a photocopier to print professional-quality text and graphics. Heat fuses a fine dark powder, called toner, onto paper to create text and images.

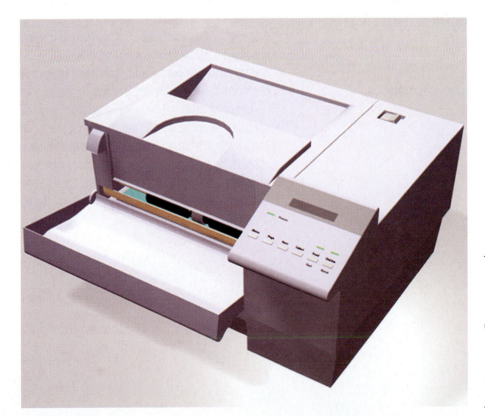

Video display adapters can use special graphics chips called accelerated video adapters to increase the speed at which images are displayed.

Communicating with computers: prompts, wizards, and command-line interfaces

To effectively use the computer, you must communicate with it; you must tell the computer what tasks to perform, and you must accurately interpret the information the computer provides to you. The means by which humans and computers communicate is referred to as the **user interface**. Through the user interface, the computer accepts your input and presents you with output. This output provides you with the results of processing, confirms the completion of the processing, or indicates that data was stored. Three means of communicating with computers are with prompts, wizards, and command-line interfaces.

☞ Prompts: A **prompt** is a message displayed by the computer that asks for input from the user. Some prompts, such as "Enter your name:," are helpful and easy to understand, even for beginners. Other prompts, like A:\>, are less helpful. In response to a computer prompt, you enter the requested information or follow the instruction.

　　A sequence of prompts is sometimes used to develop a user interface called a **prompted dialog**. In a prompted dialog, a sort of conversation takes place between the computer and user.

☞ Wizards: Current commercial software tends to use "wizards" instead of prompted dialogs. A **wizard** is a sequence of screens that direct you through multi-step software tasks such as creating a graph, a list of business contacts, or a fax cover sheet. Wizards, like the one in Figure 1-13, use graphics and dialog boxes (discussed in the next lesson) to help explain the prompts and allow users to back up and change their responses.

☞ Commands: A **command** is an instruction you input to tell the computer to carry out a task. An interface that requires the user to type in commands is referred to as a **command-line user interface**. Each word in a command results in a specific action by the computer.

　　The commands you input must conform to a specific syntax. **Syntax** specifies the sequence and punctuation for command words, parameters, and switches. If you misspell a command word, leave out required punctuation, or type the command words out of order, you will get an **error message** or **syntax error**. When you get an error message or syntax error, you must figure out what is wrong with the command and retype it correctly.

FIGURE 1-13: *Using a wizard to make a list of business clients*

This wizard prompts you at each step. This step asks you to decide what information you want to maintain for each business contact.

This wizard in the Microsoft Works software helps you set up a list of business contacts.

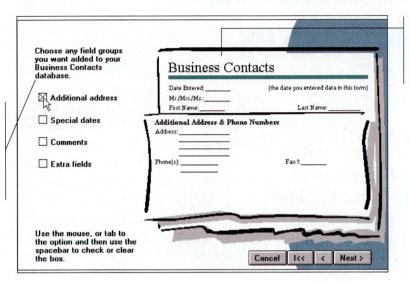

This step asks you to decide how you want the list to look. You can select from several professionally designed styles.

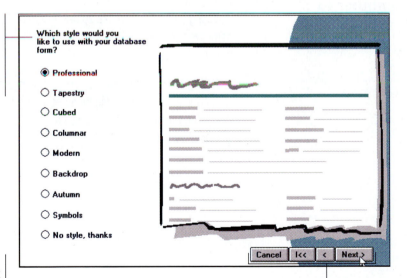

The wizard lets you move forward or back up and change your responses until the business contacts list is set up to your satisfaction.

A classic example of a poorly designed computer prompt is the screen message, "Press any key to continue." Apparently, some users have become frustrated when they can't find a key on the keyboard labeled "Any Key!"

If you forget the correct command word or punctuation, or if you find yourself using an unfamiliar command-line user interface, you may be able to find help right on the computer. Type HELP and press the [Enter] key to access help built into the software.

Communicating with computers: menus and dialog boxes

Menus and dialog boxes were developed as a response to the difficulties many people experienced trying to remember the command words and syntax for command-line user interfaces. Menus and dialog boxes are popular because when you use them, you do not have to remember command words. You simply choose the command you want from a menu or enter information in a dialog box specific to the task you want the computer to complete.

- A **menu** displays a list of commands or options. Each line of the menu is a command and is referred to as a **menu option** or a **menu item**. Figure 1-14 shows you how to use a menu.

    You might wonder how a menu can present all the commands you want to input. Obviously, there are many possibilities for combining command words, so there could be hundreds of menu options. Two methods are generally used to present a reasonably sized list of menu options. One method uses a menu hierarchy. The other method uses a dialog box.

- A **hierarchy** is an organization of things ranked one above the other. For example, a business might show the hierarchy of its employees on an organizational chart. A **menu hierarchy**, as the name implies, arranges menus in a hierarchical structure. After you make a selection from one menu, a submenu appears, and you can make additional choices by selecting an option from the submenu. Some software has a fairly complex menu hierarchy, making it difficult to remember how to find a particular menu option.

- A **dialog box** displays the options associated with a command. Instead of leading to a submenu, some menu options lead to a dialog box. You fill in the dialog box to indicate specifically how you want the command carried out, as shown in Figure 1-15.

FIGURE 1-14: *Using menus from a menu bar*

The **menu bar** is usually at the top of the screen. The menu bar for this software package includes File, Edit, View, Insert, Format, and Help menus. To use this pull-down menu, you first select which menu you want to use from a menu bar.

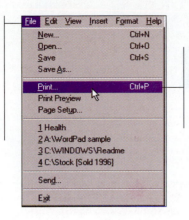

You select the option you want by using the mouse or keyboard. When a menu option is selected, it is highlighted on the screen.

Although a dialog box appears in conjunction with a menu, it is really a different type of user interface element. It combines the characteristics of both menus and prompts.

FIGURE 1-15: *Using a dialog box*

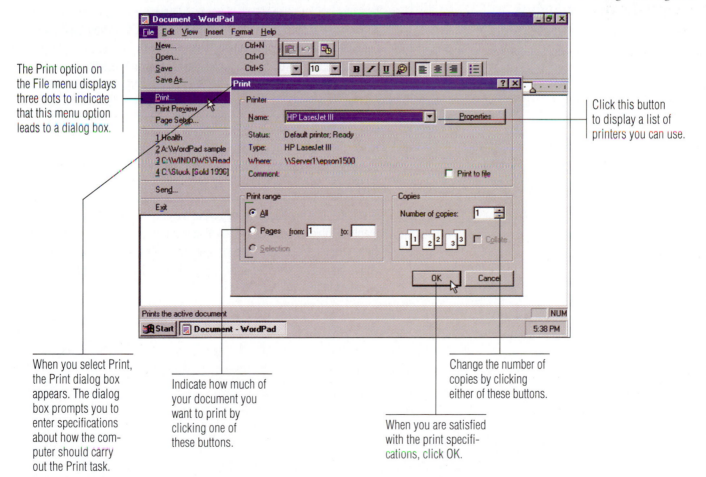

The Print option on the File menu displays three dots to indicate that this menu option leads to a dialog box.

Click this button to display a list of printers you can use.

When you select Print, the Print dialog box appears. The dialog box prompts you to enter specifications about how the computer should carry out the Print task.

Indicate how much of your document you want to print by clicking one of these buttons.

Change the number of copies by clicking either of these buttons.

When you are satisfied with the print specifications, click OK.

Communicating with computers: graphical user interfaces

GRAPHICAL USER INTERFACES OR GUIs (pronounced "gooies") are found on most of today's micro-computers. GUIs are based on the philosophy that people can use computers intuitively—that is, with minimal training—if they can manipulate on-screen objects that represent tasks or commands.

Graphical objects are key elements of GUIs. A graphical object is a small picture on the screen that you can manipulate using a mouse or other input device. Each graphical object represents a computer task, command, or a real-world object. You show the computer what you want it to do by manipulating an object instead of entering commands or selecting menu options. Graphical objects are explained in Figure 1-16.

An example of manipulating on-screen objects is the way you delete a document using Windows 95. The documents you create are represented by icons that look like sheets of paper. A Recycle Bin represents the place where you put documents you no longer want. Suppose you used your computer to write a report named "Sport Statistics," but you no longer need the report stored on your computer system. You use the mouse to drag the Sport Statistics icon to the Recycle Bin and erase the report from your computer system, as explained in Figure 1-17.

Most graphical user interfaces are based on a metaphor in which computer components are represented by real-world objects. For example, a user interface using a **desktop metaphor** might represent documents as file folders and storage as a filing cabinet.

Graphical user interfaces often contain menus and prompts in addition to graphical objects because graphical user interface designers found it difficult to design icons and tools for every possible task, command, and option you might want to perform. Figure 1-18 shows some of these elements in the Windows 95 interface.

FIGURE 1-16: *Graphical objects*

► A **window** usually contains a specific piece of work. For example, a window might contain a document you are typing or a picture you are drawing. You can think of windows as work areas, analogous to different documents and books that you might have open on your desk. Just as you switch between the documents and books you have on your desk, you can switch between windows on the computer screen to work on different tasks.

A **button** helps you make a selection. Some buttons are labeled with pictures. These buttons are sometimes referred to as **tools**. When you click a button, sometimes its appearance changes to indicate that it has been activated.

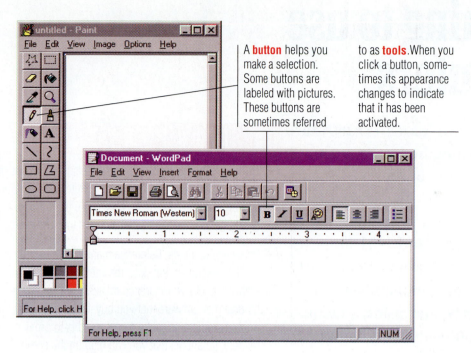

FIGURE 1-17: *Manipulating on-screen objects*

An **icon** is a small picture that represents an object. When you select an icon, you indicate to the computer that you want to manipulate the object.

A selected icon is highlighted. The Sports Statistics icon on the left is selected, so it is highlighted with dark blue.

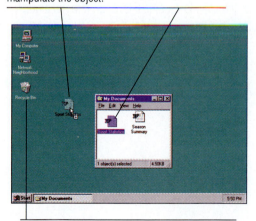

The Sport Statistics document is no longer needed. Use the mouse to drag the Sport Statistics document icon to the

Recycle Bin. Once it is placed in the Recycle Bin, the document will no longer appear in the document window.

FIGURE 1-18: *The Windows 95 GUI*

The **menu bar** displays menu titles. Selecting a menu title displays its pull-down menu.

The **toolbars** display buttons or tools that provide shortcuts to the commands on the menus.

This **wizard** appears when you click the ChartWizard button. The ChartWizard escorts you through the steps to create a chart or graph.

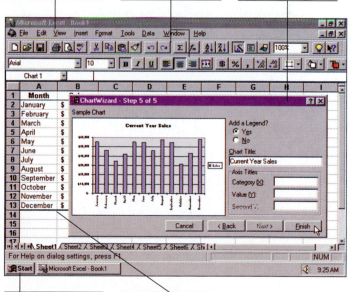

The **taskbar** contains buttons that show you which software programs you are using.

A **window** in the background contains the data for the chart.

Learning to use computers

PART OF LEARNING ABOUT COMPUTER systems is learning how to use computer systems. One of the most frequent computer activities you will perform is starting a program. Figures 1-19, 1-20, and 1-21 illustrate the different ways you can start a program—using commands, using graphical objects, and using a menu.

If, when you use your computer system, you have difficulty, you can find "how to" information about installing computer hardware and using computer software in books, on your computer screen, on videotapes, and on audio cassettes. These books, tapes, and so forth are referred to as "resources." To use these resources effectively, you need to know they exist, you need to know where to find them, and you need to develop some strategies for applying the information they contain. Let's take a look at some of the resources available to you.

IN MORE DETAIL

⊶ On-line help: The term "on-line" refers to resources that are immediately available on your computer screen. Reference information is frequently available as **on-line help**, accessible from a Help menu, a button on the toolbar, or by typing HELP at a command-line prompt.

⊶ Reference manuals: Reference manuals are usually printed books or on-line resources that describe each feature of a hardware device or software package. Reference manuals are usually included with the hardware or software that you buy. Most often, reference manuals are printed documents, but a recent trend is to provide computer-based reference manuals that you can read on the computer screen. Computer-based reference manuals are extensive and are often distributed on CD-ROMs.

You can also find independent publishers who produce reference manuals for popular hardware and, particularly, for popular software. You might want to purchase one of these reference manuals if it is easier to understand or better organized than the manual included with the hardware or software you purchased.

A reference manual is typically organized by features, rather than in the lesson format used by tutorials. Do not assume that you should read a reference manual from cover to cover. Instead, leaf through it to get a quick overview of all the features.

FIGURE 1-19: *Starting Microsoft Works using commands*

▶ To start Microsoft Works using the DOS command-line user interface, you need to know the name of the program. In this case, the computer calls Microsoft Works "works." At the DOS prompt, C: type works, then press Enter.

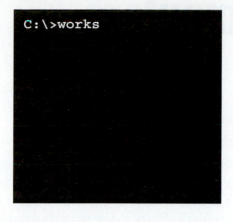

```
C:\>works
```

FIGURE 1-20: *Starting Microsoft Works using graphical objects*

▶ To start Microsoft Works using the Windows 3.1 user interface, you move the pointer to the Microsoft Works graphical object and double-click the left mouse button.

FIGURE 1-21: *Starting Microsoft Works using menus*

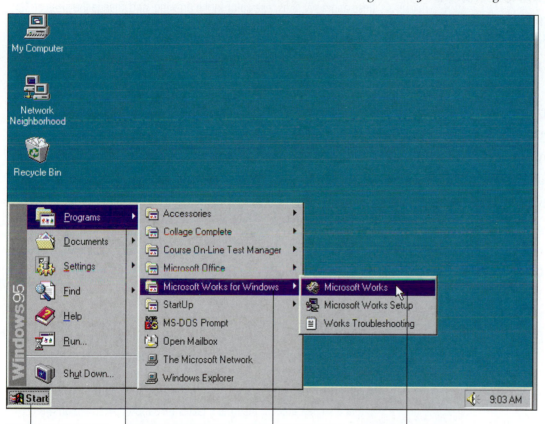

To start Microsoft Works using the Windows 95 interface, use the mouse to move the pointer to the Start button and click to view a menu of categories.

Use the mouse to move the pointer to the Programs menu item to display a list of program folders.

Use the mouse to move the pointer to the Microsoft Works for Windows folder to display the contents of the Microsoft Works folder.

Use the mouse to move the pointer to Microsoft Works and click to start the program.

QUICK TIP

Public libraries, bookstores, and newsstands have computer trade magazines that provide interesting articles and current, pertinent tips about computers. The information in these magazines is often presented in non-technical, easy-to-use language.

FYI

Use a reference manual to find out if a feature exists or to find out how to use a feature. When you use a reference manual, you should first check the table of contents or index to locate the information you need, then turn to the appropriate section and read it carefully.

Learning to use computers, continued

If you are an adventurous learner, you might enjoy exploring software applications without referring to resources such as the ones previously described. Graphical and menu-driven user interfaces make this sort of exploration possible, as do interfaces that include on-line help. Figure 1-22 shows how you access on-line help for Microsoft Windows 95.

However, to learn more about all the features of a particular software package, it is worthwhile to consider one of these: tutorial software packages, courses, or support line services.

○━ Tutorials: A **tutorial** is a guided, step-by-step learning experience. Usually this learning experience teaches you the generic skills you need to use specific hardware or software. For example, suppose you purchase software to create pictures, and the first thing you want to draw is your company logo. When you use a tutorial that teaches you how to create a drawing on the computer, you learn how to do such things as draw straight lines and wavy lines, use color in the drawing, and change the sizes of the pictures you draw. The tutorial does not teach you exactly how to draw your company logo; therefore, you need to think about how you can generalize the skills you are learning so you can apply them to other tasks.

Tutorials might be produced by the publisher of the software you want to use or by independent publishers. You can purchase tutorials at many bookstores and computer stores. Tutorials come in a variety of forms, as listed in Table 1-1.

○━ Courses: Another approach to learning how to use computers is to take a course. Because you're reading this book, you are probably enrolled in an introductory computer course. Courses are available from schools, manufacturers, and private training firms and might last from several hours to several months. Courses about software packages tend to be laboratory-based with an instructor leading you through steps. Some courses might be lecture only, however. You might want to ask about the course format before you register.

○━ Support line of a software or hardware company: A **support line** is a service offered over the phone by a hardware manufacturer or software publisher to customers who have questions about how to use a software or hardware product. Sometimes these support line calls are toll-free; sometimes they are not. In addition to paying for the phone call, you might also pay a fee for the time it takes the support person to answer your question.

○━ No one resource can ever teach you all you need to know about using computers or everything about one software package. Don't expect to figure things out in a flash of inspiration! But remember, many resources are available to help you learn how to use computers. Take time to seek those resources that suit your budget, schedule, and learning style. One of the most important skills you can develop as a computer user is the ability to figure out how to do new computing tasks on your own.

FIGURE 1-22: *Using on-line Help for the Windows 95 software*

In Windows 95 software, Help is available on the menu bar or from the Start button. Help appears in a Help window.

Help has three sections: Contents, Index, and Find. To select the section you want, click one of the tabs.

The Contents section of Help, look through the list of "books." Each book covers a help subject.

Once you open a Help book, you will see a list of specific Help topics. Click the topic you want, then click Display.

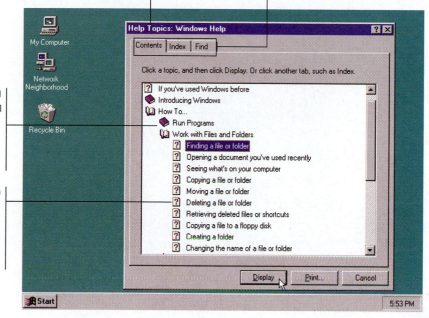

QUICK TIP

If you run into a problem and are pressed for time, the best course of action might be to ask an expert. You might have a friend who knows a lot about computers; or on the job, you might know a computer "guru." These are both good sources of information, as long as you don't overuse them.

TABLE 1-1: *Reference resources*

RESOURCE		DESCRIPTION
Printed tutorial		Provides printed step-by-step instructions. To use a printed tutorial, you read how to do a step, then you try to do it on the computer. In the last few years, computer-based tutorials have become much more widespread.
Computer-based tutorial		Provides a simulation of the hardware or software and displays tutorial instructions in boxes or windows on the screen. Computer-based tutorials have an advantage over their printed counterparts because they can demonstrate procedures using computer animation.
Audio tutorial		Verbally walks you through the steps of the tutorial. An advantage to this type of tutorial is that you do not have to read instructions. You do have to stop the tutorial and rewind, however, if you do not hear or understand the instructions. You might like audio tutorials if you easily retain information presented in lectures.
Video tutorial		Visually illustrates how the software or hardware works. Some video tutorials are designed so that you watch them, take notes, then try the steps on the computer later. Other video tutorials are designed to be used while you are sitting at the computer. As with audio tutorials, you can stop and rewind video tutorials if you miss something.

Concepts Review

Label each element shown in Figure 1-23.

1. _____

2. _____

3. _____

4. _____

5. _____

6. _____

7. _____

8. _____

9. _____

10. _____

Match each statement with the term it describes:

11. ____ Input

12. ____ Processing

13. ____ Terminal

14. ____ Mouse

15. ____ Mainframe

a. Systematic actions a computer uses to manipulate data

b. A pointing device used to input data

c. The symbols processed by a computer

d. Category of computer

e. Resembles a microcomputer but does not have any processing capability

Fill in the best answer:

16. The four functions performed by a computer are
_____, _____, _____,
and _____.

17. The computer puts data temporarily in _____
while the data is waiting to be processed.

18. When data is not needed for processing, the computer
puts it in _____.

19. Most microcomputers are equipped with a(n)
_____ as the primary input device and a(n)
_____ as the primary output device.

20. If your organization wants to provide processing for more
than 200 users and reliability, security, and centralized
control are necessary, a(n) _____ computer
would best meet your needs.

21. An IBM computer is _____ with a Compaq computer because it operates in essentially the same way.

22. A(n) _____, such as "Enter your name:," is one
way a computer can tell the user what to do.

23. Instead of prompted dialogs, today's software tends to use
_____ to direct a user through multi-step software tasks, such as creating a graph or creating a fax
cover sheet.

24. Most _____ are based on a metaphor in which
computer components are represented by real-world
objects, such as a desktop metaphor in which
documents are represented by folder icons.

25. You can use the _____ key and the
_____ key in conjunction with letter keys
instead of using the mouse to control menus.

INDEPENDENT CHALLENGE 1

To complete this independent challenge:

Draw a sketch of a computer system in your computer lab,
home, or office. Be sure to draw all of the components of the
computer system (not just the computer). Once your sketch is
complete, do the following:

1. Title the sketch appropriately, for example, "My Computer
at Home."

2. List its brand name and model number, for example, "Dell
486/50."

3. Label the following components, if applicable:

monitor	screen	keyboard
3.5" disk drive	5.25" disk drive	hard drive light
CD-ROM drive	power switch	power light
system unit	pointing device	speakers
	printer	modem

INDEPENDENT CHALLENGE 2

Look in a computer magazine and photocopy one ad for each of the following types of microcomputer: desktop, tower, notebook, and PDA.

To complete this independent challenge:

For each advertisement that you selected, label each component and indicate if it is an input, output, processing, or storage device on the computer. See Independent Challenge 1 for
a list of the available components.

INDEPENDENT CHALLENGE 3

Do this project only if your school has a computer network for student use. If the network requires a user ID and password, get them. Learn how to log in. Your school might have a short tutorial that teaches you how to use the network, or your instructor might provide a demonstration.

To complete this independent challenge:

Write a one- to two-page step-by-step tutorial on how to log into the network. Your tutorial should include the following:

1. A title

2. An introductory paragraph explaining where the network is located, who can access it, and how students can get a user ID and password

3. Numbered steps to log into the network (if your lab policy requires that you turn on the computer each time you log in, you should include instructions for doing this in your tutorial)

4. Numbered steps for logging out of the network

INDEPENDENT CHALLENGE 4

Do this project only if your school provides you with access to the Internet. The Internet is a worldwide computer network that provides access to an astonishing variety of information. The Internet can be useful right from the start of this course. Several of the end-of-chapter projects refer you to information resources on the Internet. If you would like to use the Internet for these projects, this is a good time to get started.

There are several software tools to help you use the Internet, such as Mosaic, Netscape, and Lynx. It is not possible to cover all these software tools here. Therefore, this is an exploratory project that you can accomplish with the help of your instructor or with a tutorial prepared by your school.

To complete this independent challenge:

Find out how to use the Internet at your school and then answer the following questions:

1. What is the name of the software tool you use to access the Internet?

2. How do you access the "home page" for your school?

3. What other locations or "sites" are available from your home page? List at least five. How do you get to these other sites?

4. How can you keep track of where you have been on the Internet? (In other words, is there a way to bookmark sites?)

5. When you are finished browsing on the Internet, how do you quit?

Software, Data Storage, and the Internet

Unit 2

THE QUEST FOR MULTIPURPOSE MACHINES HAS always challenged inventors. The computer is the most successful and versatile machine in history. A computer's versatility is possible because of **software**. In this unit you will learn how a computer uses software. You will learn the difference between system software and application software, learn to identify the functions of operating systems, and find out about trends in multimedia computing. The unit explains how computers store and retrieve data and provides you with a practical foundation for using a computer to manage your own data. The availability of reasonably priced software and hardware designed for microcomputer networks ushered in a new era of computing, which increasingly provides ways for people to collaborate, communicate, and interact. This unit also helps you understand how computer networks and electronic mail works. The unit concludes with a discussion of the Internet.

OBJECTIVES

Understand computer software basics

Define and recognize operating systems

Understand computer files

Define storage technology

Understand multimedia computing

Define computer networks

Explore electronic mail (e-mail)

Tour the information highway

Understand how the Internet works

Understanding computer software basics

COMPUTER SOFTWARE DETERMINES what a computer can do; and in a sense, it transforms a computer from one kind of machine to another — from a drafting station to a typesetting machine, from a flight simulator to a calculator, from a filing system to a music studio, and so on. The distinction between software, programs, and data is important. This lesson defines the terms *computer program, data,* and *software.*

IN MORE DETAIL

○—☞ A **computer program** is a set of detailed, step-by-step instructions that tell a computer how to solve a problem or carry out a task. The steps in a computer program are written in a language that the computer can interpret or "understand." As you read through the simple computer program in Figure 2-1, notice the number of steps required to perform a relatively simple calculation. At one time, computer users had to invest the time and expense of writing many of their own programs. Today, people rarely write computer programs for their personal computers, preferring to select from thousands of commercially written programs.

○—☞ **Data** are the words, numbers, and graphics that describe people, events, things, and ideas. Data can be included in the software, like the data for a dictionary in a word processing program, and you can create data such as numbers you provide for a graph.

○—☞ **Software** is a basic part of a computer system, but "software" is a term that has more than one definition. In the early days of the computer industry, it became popular to use the term "software" for all the non-hardware components of a computer. In this context, software referred to computer programs and to the data used by the programs. In practice, the term "software" is usually used to describe a commercial product as shown in Figure 2-2, which might include more than a single program and might also include data.

In this textbook, we define **software** as instructions and associated data, stored in electronic format, that direct the computer to accomplish a task. Under this definition, computer software may include more than one computer program, if those programs work together to carry out a task. Also under this definition, software can include data, but data alone is not software. For example, word processing software might include the data for a dictionary, but the data *you create* using a word processor is not referred to as software.

Software categories

There are two major categories of software: system software and application software. **System software** helps the computer carry out its basic operating tasks. **Application software** helps the human user carry out a task. System software and application software are further divided into subcategories. Use Figure 2-3 to help you understand the differences between system and application software.

The first section of the program states that there are 12 inches in a foot and 2.54 centimeters in an inch.

The var, or variable, section lists the factors in the problem that might change each time you use the program.

When you use the program, it asks you to enter the length you want to convert.

The program converts the feet and inches you entered into inches.

```
program Conversion(input, output);
const
   { inchesPerFoot = 12;
     centimetersPerInch = 2.54;
   { var
       feet, inches, lengthInInches: integer;
       centimeters: real;
begin
   write('What is the length in feet and inches?');
   readln(feet, inches);
   lengthInInches :=inchesPerFoot * feet + inches;
   centimeters :=centimetersPerInch * lengthInInches;
   writeln('The length in centimeters is ', centimeters:1:2)
end.
```

Next, the program converts the inches into centimeters.

The program then displays the answer.

QUICK TIP

"Software" is a plural noun, so there is no such thing as "softwares." Use the term "software package" when referring to a particular example of software.

FIGURE 2-2: *A software product*

A **software** package contains disks and a reference manual.

The disks contain **programs**. For example, some of the programs that might be included in a word processor are a

text editor, printing routines, and grammar checker.
   The disks might also contain **data** such as a dictionary

of words for the spell checker or a collection of pictures for adding visual interest to documents.

FIGURE 2-3: *Software categories*

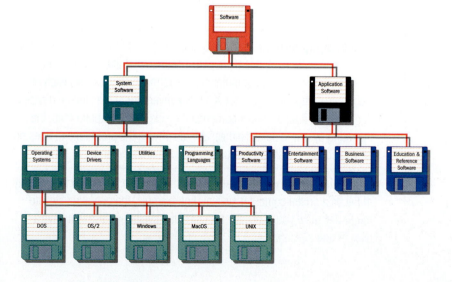

FYI

Remember the key difference between system software and application software: system software helps the *computer*; application software helps *you*.

Defining and recognizing operating systems

An **OPERATING SYSTEM** IS THE software that controls the computer's use of its hardware resources such as memory and disk storage space. An operating system works like an air traffic controller to coordinate the activities within the computer. Just as an airport cannot function without air traffic controllers, a computer cannot function without an operating system. Figure 2-4 helps you envision the relationship between your computer hardware, the operating system, and application software.

IN MORE DETAIL

- The operating system works as a liaison between the computer hardware and application software. An operating system helps you start an application, then it works "behind the scenes" while the application software is running to perform tasks essential to the efficient functioning of the computer system. Refer to Figure 2-5 to discover more details about what an operating system does.

- **Control basic input and output**: an operating system controls the flow of data into and out of the computer, as well as the flow of data to and from peripheral devices. It routes your input to areas of the computer where it can be processed and routes output to the screen, a printer, or any other output device you request.

- **Ensure adequate space**: an operating system ensures that adequate space is available for each program that is running and makes sure that each processor quickly performs each program instruction. And if you want to run two or more programs at a time—a process called multi-tasking—the operating system ensures that each program has adequate space and run time.

- **Allocate system resources**: an operating system allocates system resources so programs run smoothly. A system resource is part of a computer system, such as a disk drive, memory, printer, or processor time, that can be used by a computer program.

- **Manage storage space**: an operating system keeps track of the data stored on disks and CD-ROMs. Think of your disks as filing cabinets, your data as papers stored in file folders, and the operating system as the filing clerk. The filing clerk takes care of filing a folder when you finish using it. When you need something from your filing cabinet, you ask the filing clerk to get it. The filing clerk knows where to find the folder.

- **Detect equipment failure**: an operating system monitors the status of critical computer components to detect failures that affect processing. When you turn on your computer, the operating system checks each of the electronic components and takes a quick inventory of the storage devices. For example, if an electrical component inside your computer fails, the operating system displays a message identifying the problem and does not let you continue with the computing session until the problem is fixed.

- **Maintain security**: an operating system also helps maintain the security of the data on the computer system. For example, the operating system might not allow you to access the computer system unless you have a user ID and a password.

FIGURE 2-4: *The relationship among hardware, operating system, and application software*

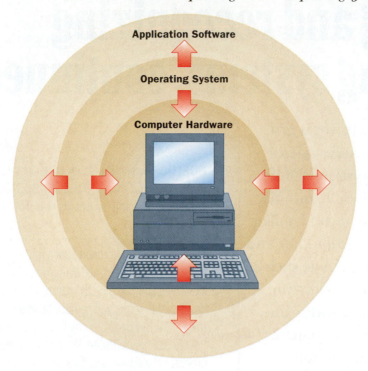

Application Software

Operating System

Computer Hardware

FIGURE 2-5: *Operating system functions*

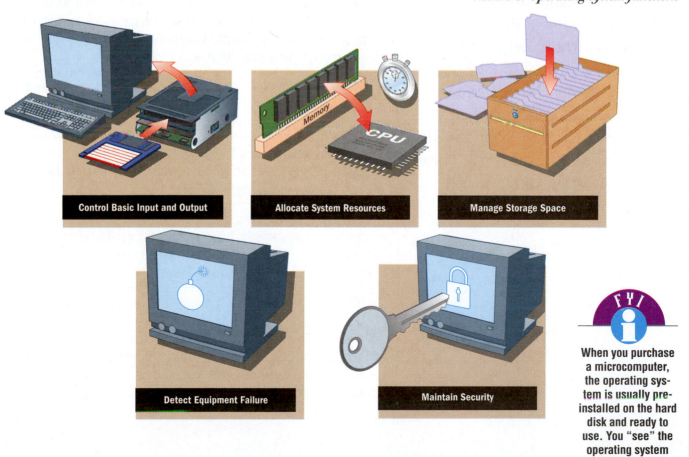

Control Basic Input and Output

Allocate System Resources

Manage Storage Space

Detect Equipment Failure

Maintain Security

When you purchase a microcomputer, the operating system is usually pre-installed on the hard disk and ready to use. You "see" the operating system each time you turn on your computer.

Defining and recognizing operating systems, continued

YOU MIGHT BE FAMILIAR WITH THE names of the most popular microcomputer operating systems: DOS, Microsoft Windows, OS/2, and Mac OS. You are less likely to be familiar with the names of minicomputer and mainframe operating systems such as UNIX, VMS, and MVS. Operating systems for micro, mini, and mainframe computers perform many similar tasks. How can you tell which operating system your computer uses? Many microcomputer users can recognize an operating system by looking at the first screen that appears when they turn the computer on or by recognizing the operating system prompt. Figure 2-6 shows screens for commonly used operating systems, reviewing them will help you recognize these operating systems when you encounter them in the future.

IN MORE DETAIL

DOS: DOS, which stands for Disk Operating System, is marketed under the trade names PC-DOS and MS-DOS. Both PC-DOS and MS-DOS were developed primarily by Microsoft Corporation and are essentially the same operating system.

Windows 3.1: Microsoft took a more graphical approach to operating systems when it designed Windows. Microsoft Windows 3.1 provides icons that you can directly manipulate on the screen using a pointing device, and menus you can use to issue commands. The applications you use with Windows 3.1 all have a consistent look, so it is easy to learn how to use new software. Windows 3.1 also lets you run more than one program at a time in separate windows on the screen, and lets you easily transfer data between them. While using Windows 3.1, you can still run DOS software.

Windows 95: Microsoft introduced a new version of Windows in 1995 which offers better operating efficiency than Windows 3.1. In addition to programs designed specially for Windows 95, the operating system also runs software designed for Windows 3.1 and DOS.

Windows NT: The network version of the Windows operating system is Windows NT. With Windows NT you can connect your computer to other computers to share software programs and data.

OS/2: OS/2 was designed jointly by Microsoft and IBM. If your computer uses OS/2, you can use most DOS and Windows software, as well as software designed specifically for OS/2.

Mac OS: Apple Computer, Inc. defined a new direction in operating system user interfaces that became an industry standard with its Macintosh computer. The Macintosh Operating System is referred to as Mac OS or by its version number, for example, System 7.

UNIX: UNIX is an operating system that was developed by AT&T's Bell Laboratories in 1969 and is now used as one of the foundation technologies on the information superhighway. UNIX was originally designed for minicomputers, but is now available for microcomputers and mainframes. Many versions of UNIX exist, such as AIX from IBM, XENIX from Microsoft, and ULTRIX from Digital Equipment Corporation.

FIGURE 2-6: *Microcomputer operating systems*

The DOS prompt is a distinguishing feature of MS DOS and PC DOS.

The cursor shows your place on the screen.

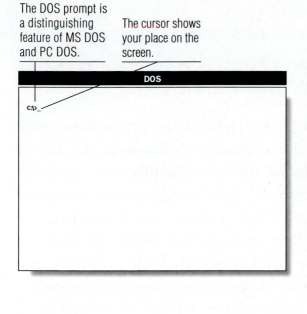

DOS

c:\>_

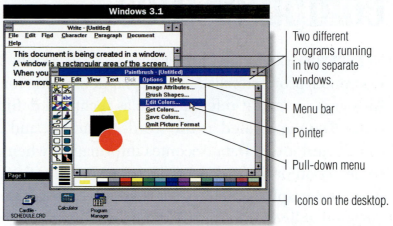

Windows 3.1

Write - [Untitled]
File   Edit   Find   Character   Paragraph   Document
Help

This document is being created in a window.
A window is a rectangular area of the screen.
When you
have more

Paintbrush - [Untitled]
File   Edit   View   Text   Pick   Options   Help

Image Attributes...
Brush Shapes...
Edit Colors...
Get Colors...
Save Colors...
Omit Picture Format

Page 1

Cardfile   Calculator   Program
SCHEDULE.CRD   Manager

Two different programs running in two separate windows.

Menu bar

Pointer

Pull-down menu

Icons on the desktop.

My Computer icon   Disk drive icon   Title bar   Menu bar

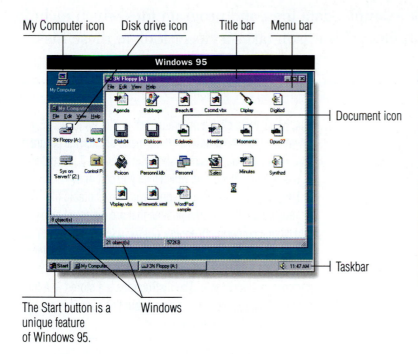

Windows 95

3½ Floppy (A:)
File   Edit   View   Help

Agenda   Babbage   Beach.fl   Cscmd.vbx   Ctplay   Digitzd

Disk04   Diskicon   Edelweis   Meeting   Moonsnta   Opus27

Pcicon   Personnl.kdb   Personnl   Sales   Minutes   Synthzd

Vtplay.vbx   Wmnwork.wmf   WordPad sample

My Computer
File   Edit   View   Help

3½ Floppy (A:)   Disk_0

Sys on   Control P.
'Server1' (Z:)

0 object(s)

21 object(s)   572KB

Start   My Computer   3½ Floppy (A:)   11:47 AM

Document icon

Taskbar

The Start button is a unique feature of Windows 95.

Windows

Menu bar   File folder icons

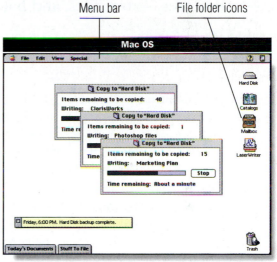

Mac OS

File   Edit   View   Special

Copy to "Hard Disk"
Items remaining to be copied: 40
Writing: ClarisWorks
Time r

Copy to "Hard Disk"
Items remaining to be copied: 1
Writing: Photoshop files

Copy to "Hard Disk"
Items remaining to be copied: 15
Writing: Marketing Plan
Stop
Time remaining: About a minute

Friday, 6:00 PM. Hard Disk backup complete.

Today's Documents   Stuff To File

Hard Disk

Catalogs

Mailbox

LaserWriter

Trash

All the operating systems discussed, except DOS, use some level of graphical user interface and support multitasking, networking, and electronic mail.

Understanding computer files

IN EVERYDAY CONVERSATION, PEOPLE USE THE TERMS *DATA* AND *INFORMATION* INTERCHANGEABLY. Computer professionals have special definitions for the terms *data, information,* and *file.* Although we might refer to these as technical definitions, they are not difficult to understand. **Data** is defined as the words, numbers, and graphics that describe people, events, things, and ideas. Data becomes information when you use it as the basis for initiating some action or for making a decision. **Information**, then, is defined as the words, numbers, and graphics used as the basis for human actions and decisions. A **file** is defined as a named collection of program instructions or data that exists on a storage medium such as a hard disk, a floppy disk, or a CD-ROM.

There are several kinds of files. For example, data files, and program files which include executable files, source files, and batch files. This lesson takes a closer look at these files.

IN MORE DETAIL

Data Files: A **data file** contains words, numbers, and pictures that you can view, edit, save, send, and print. Typically, you create data files when you use application software. For example, you create a data file when you store a document you have written using word processing software or when you store a picture you have drawn using graphics software.

You probably won't create all the data files you use; you might receive data files as part of a software package you purchase. For example, word processing software often includes a dictionary data file that contains a list of words the software uses to check spelling.

Executable Files: An **executable file** contains the instructions that tell a computer how to perform a specific task. For example, the word processing program that tells your computer how to display and print text is stored on disk as an executable file. Other executable files on your computer system include the operating system, utilities, and programs for application software.

To use some executable files, you *run* them. Most operating systems help you identify the executable files you can run. DOS uses part of the filename to indicate an executable file. To run an executable file in DOS you type the file name of the program; in Windows 3.1 you click a program icon, and in Windows 95 you can either select the program from a menu or click the program icon. The Windows 95 screen shown in Figure 2-7 illustrates the use of icons to indicate which files you can run.

The programs you run are one type of executable file. Your computer also has executable files that are executed at the request of a computer program, not the user. For example, a word processing program might request that the computer use an executable file called GRAMMAR.DLL to check the grammar in a document. The instructions are stored in a format that the computer can interpret, but this format is not designed to be readable to humans.

Source Files: A **source file** contains instructions that a computer user can understand and that must be translated before a computer can execute them. A computer user can request that a specific source file be run. The computer does the translation, so it seems as if the source program is being executed just like an executable file. But this is not the case; behind the scenes, a translation program is busy converting the source program into commands the computer can execute.

FIGURE 2-7: *Program icons*

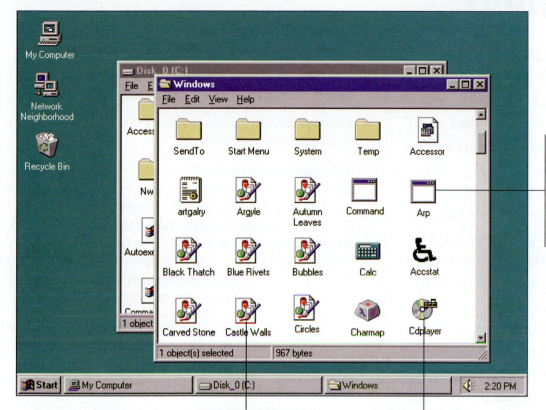

Some files you can run do not have unique icons. Instead, they use a "generic" icon of a blank window. The label indicates the name of the file.

Some files are represented by icons that look like pages. These icons represent data files.

Many of the files you can run are indicated by unique icons. Each icon has a label that tells you the name of the application.

You can think of executable files as *active*: the instructions stored in the file cause the computer to do something. Think of data files as *passive*: the computer processes the data, but the data generally does not direct the process.

Batch files

One type of source file is a batch file. A **batch file** is a series of operating system commands that you use to automate tasks you want the operating system to perform. When you first turn on an IBM-compatible computer, it looks for a batch file called AUTOEXEC.BAT. If it finds this file, the computer automatically executes any instructions the file contains. Usually the AUTOEXEC.BAT file contains instructions that customize your computer configuration. A batch file, such as AUTOEXEC.BAT, contains instructions that can be read and modified by computer users. The commands in a batch file must go through a translation process before they can be executed.

Defining storage technology

YOUR COMPUTER SYSTEM MIGHT contain hundreds, or even thousands, of files stored on disks and storage devices. To keep track of all these files, the computer has a filing system that is maintained by the operating system. Once you know how the operating system manages your computer's filing system, you can use it effectively to store and retrieve files. **Logical storage** is a conceptual model of the way data is stored on your disk. This logical view of storage is a convenient mental model that helps you understand the computer's filing system; however, it is not how the data is actually stored. **Physical storage** refers to how data is actually stored on the physical disk. Take a closer look at storage technology and what it means.

IN MORE DETAIL

- **Storage technology** refers to a storage device and the media it uses.

- A **storage medium** (storage *media* is the plural) is the disk, tape, paper, or other substance that contains data.

- A **storage device** is the mechanical apparatus such as a disk drive that records and retrieves the data from the storage medium. Most computers have more than one storage device that the operating system uses to store files. Each storage device is identified by a letter and a colon. Floppy disk drives are usually identified as A: and B:. The hard disk drive is usually identified as C:. Additional storage devices can be assigned letters from D: through Z:. Figure 2-8 shows some microcomputer configurations and the letters typically assigned to their storage devices.

- The process of storing data is often referred to as **writing data** or **saving a file**, because the storage device *writes* the data on the storage medium to save it for later use.

- The process of retrieving data is often referred to as **reading data**, **loading data**, or **opening a file**. The terms *reading data* and *writing data* are often associated with mainframe applications. The terms *save* and *open* are standard Windows terminology.

- **Storage Specifications**: Storage technology comparisons are often based on storage capacity and speed. Therefore, knowing the characteristics of a storage device or storage medium helps you determine which one is best for a particular task.

- **Storage capacity** is the maximum amount of data that can be stored on a storage medium. Data is stored as bytes—each **byte** usually represents one character. Data is usually measured in kilobytes (KB), about 1024 bytes; megabytes (MB), about 1 million bytes; or gigabytes (GB), about 1 billion bytes. For example, the phrase "profit margin" requires 13 bytes of storage space because the phrase contains 13 characters including the space between the two words. When you read that the storage capacity of a computer is 850 MB, it means the hard disk on that computer can store up to 850 million bytes of information. This is equivalent to approximately 225,000 single-spaced pages of text.

FIGURE 2-8: *Storage device letter assignments*

▼ This desktop model has an impressive array of storage devices. The 3.5" floppy drive is drive A: and the 5.25" floppy drive is drive B:. The hard disk drive is C: and the CD-ROM drive is D:. The tape storage device does not have a drive letter because it is not a storage device you can use to store individual files from within your applications.

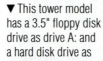

▼ This tower model has a 3.5" floppy disk drive as drive A: and a hard disk drive as drive C:. There is no drive B:, but the CD-ROM drive is drive D:.

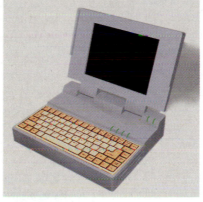

▲ This desktop model computer has a 3.5" floppy disk drive as drive A: and a 5.25" floppy disk drive as drive B:. Inside the case is the hard disk drive, drive C:.

▲ This notebook computer has one 3.5" floppy disk drive as drive A:. The hard disk drive, C:, is inside the case. There is no drive B:. Because of space restrictions it is difficult to fit many storage devices in a notebook computer.

Magnetic storage, storing data on disks and tape by magnetizing selected particles of an oxide-based surface coating and optical storage, using beams of laser light to burn pits on a CD-ROM's surface, are used for the majority of today's microcomputers.

To differentiate between physical and logical file storage, remember that physical storage refers to the way data is electronically stored on the storage medium. Logical storage refers to the metaphor you use to visualize the organization of your files.

The time it takes to get the data

Access time is the average time it takes a computer to locate data on the storage medium and read it. Access time for microcomputer storage devices, such as a disk drive, is measured in milliseconds. One **millisecond** (ms) is a thousandth of a second. When you read, for example, that disk access time is 11 ms, it means that on average, it takes the computer eleven thousandths of a second to locate and read data from the disk.

Defining Storage technology, continued

NOW THAT YOU UNDERSTAND HOW A STORAGE DEVICE STORES DATA ON A STORAGE MEDIUM, LET'S look at how files are stored. Files are stored in clusters. A **cluster** is a group of sectors and is the smallest storage unit the computer can access. The number of sectors that form a cluster depends on the type of computer. IBM-compatible computers form a cluster from two sectors. Each cluster is numbered and the operating system maintains a list of which sectors correspond to each cluster.

IN MORE DETAIL

- When the computer stores a file on a random-access storage medium, the operating system records the cluster number that contains the beginning of the file in a File Allocation Table, or FAT. The **FAT** is an operating system file that helps the computer store and retrieve files from disk storage by maintaining a list of files and their physical location on the disk. The FAT is such a crucial file that if it is damaged by a head crash or other disaster, you generally lose access to all the data stored on your disk because the list of clusters that contain files is no longer readable. This is yet another reason to have a backup of the data on your hard drive.

- When you want to store a file, the operating system looks at the FAT to see which clusters are empty. The operating system then records the data for the file in empty clusters. The cluster numbers are recorded in the FAT. The name of the new file and the number of the first cluster that contains the file data are recorded in the directory.

- A file that does not fit into a single cluster will spill over into the next adjacent or *contiguous* cluster unless that cluster already contains data. If the next cluster is full, the operating system stores the file in a nonadjacent cluster and sets up instructions called *pointers*. These "point" to each piece of the file, as shown in Figure 2-9.

- When you want to retrieve a file, the operating system looks through the directory for the filename and the number of the first cluster that contains the file data. The FAT tells the computer which clusters contain the remaining data for the file. The operating system moves the read-write head to the cluster that contains the beginning of the file and reads it. If the file is stored in more than one cluster, the read-write head must move to the next cluster to read more of the file. It takes longer to access a file stored in nonadjacent clusters than one stored in adjacent clusters because the disk or head must move farther to find the next section of the file.

- With random-access storage, files tend to become **fragmented**, that is, each file is stored in many nonadjacent clusters. Drive performance generally declines as the drive works harder to locate the clusters that contain the parts of a file. To regain peak performance, you can use a **defragmentation utility** to rearrange the files on a disk so that they are stored in adjacent clusters. Figure 2-10 explains more about fragmentation and defragmentation.

- **Data compression: Data compression** or **file compression** is a technique that reduces the size of a large file by using fewer bits to represent the data that the file contains on the disk. PKZIP, a popular data compression utility, creates files with the **.ZIP** extension that are sometimes called "zipped" files. You cannot use a compressed file directly—the file must be "unzipped" using the PKUNZIP utility. File compression is reversible by uncompressing, extracting, or expanding the file so the data can be returned to its original form. Compressing files is a convenient way to archive, back up, or transmit large files.

FIGURE 2-9: *How the FAT works*

► Each sector is listed in the FAT along with a number that indicates the status of the cluster.

Fat		
Cluster	**Status**	Comment
1	**1**	Reserved for operating system
2	**1**	Reserved for operating system
3	**4**	First cluster of Bio.Txt. Points to cluster 8 which holds more data for Bio.Txt.
4	**999**	Last cluster of Bio.Txt
5	**0**	Empty
6	**0**	Empty
7	**8**	First cluster for Jordan.Wks. Points to cluster 8 which holds more data for the Jordan.Wks file.
8	**10**	Points to cluster 10 which holds more data for the Jordan.Wks file.
9	**999**	First and last cluster containing Pick.Wps
10	**999**	Last cluster of Jordan.Wks

If status is "1" the cluster is reserved for technical files. If status is "0," the cluster is empty, so new data can be stored there. If the status is "999," the cluster contains the end of a file. Other status numbers indicate the sector that hold more data for a file.

Looking at the FAT entry for cluster 7, you see that the JORDAN.WKS file continues in cluster 8.

Looking at the FAT entry for cluster 8, you see that the JORDAN.WKS file continues in cluster 10.

The FAT entry for cluster 10 shows that this is the end of the JORDAN.WKS file. The file is stored in **non-contiguous clusters** 7, 8, and 10.

FIGURE 2-10: *Defragmenting a disk*

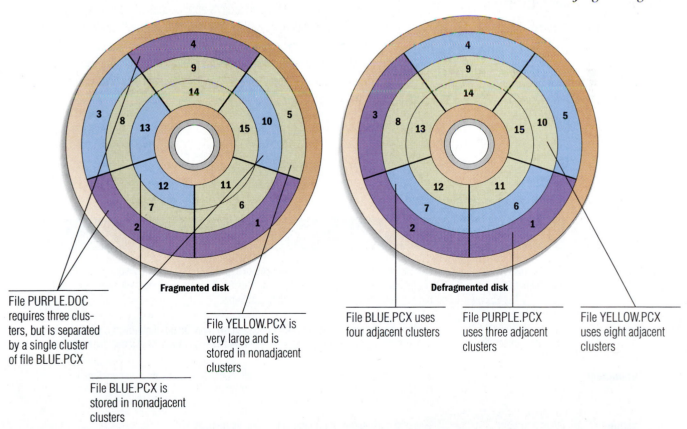

Fragmented disk

Defragmented disk

File PURPLE.DOC requires three clusters, but is separated by a single cluster of file BLUE.PCX

File YELLOW.PCX is very large and is stored in nonadjacent clusters

File BLUE.PCX is stored in nonadjacent clusters

File BLUE.PCX uses four adjacent clusters

File PURPLE.PCX uses three adjacent clusters

File YELLOW.PCX uses eight adjacent clusters

Understanding multimedia computing

THE TERM MULTIMEDIA ISN'T REALLY anything new. It refers to the integrated use of multiple media, such as slides, video tapes, audio tapes, records, CD-ROMs, and photos. Computer technology is replacing or controlling many of the technologies and media that were previously used for multimedia presentations. Advances in computer technology have made it possible to combine text, photo images, speech, music, animated sequences, and video into a single interactive computer presentation. To display realistic graphic and video, your computer system must have a high resolution monitor and a CD-ROM drive. Figure 2-11 shows a computer well-equipped for multimedia.

IN MORE DETAIL

☞ **Multimedia** is defined as an integrated collection of computer-based text, graphics, sound, animation, photo images, and video. Refer to Table 2-1 for examples of multimedia applications.

☞ Multimedia applications: One example of a multimedia application is a multimedia encyclopedia. It contains articles and pictures on a wide range of topics like a traditional encyclopedia, but a multimedia encyclopedia has more. A multimedia encyclopedia provides you with a rich selection of text, graphics, sound, animation, and video.

☞ Hypertext: **Hypertext** is a key element of many multimedia products, and has been used effectively in non-multimedia products as well. You are likely to use hypertext with many computer applications. The term hypertext was coined by Ted Nelson in 1965 to describe the idea of documents that could be linked to each other. Linked documents make it possible for a reader to jump from a passage in one document to a related passage in another document. Figure 2-12 will help you visualize a hypertext.

☞ Hypermedia: The links in today's applications often involve graphics, sound, and video, as well as text. This type of multimedia hypertext is referred to as **hypermedia.** Hypertext and hypermedia are important computer-based tools because they help you easily follow a path that makes sense to you through a large selection of text, graphical, audio, and video information.

TABLE 2-1: *A sample of multimedia applications*

TYPE	WHAT IT CAN DO	EXAMPLE
Productivity	Remind you of appointments	Use multimedia scheduler to remind you of appointments by displaying a video image of a "Personal Assistant" in one corner of the screen; "Excuse me," your PA might say, "but I believe you have an appointment in five minutes"
Business	Create a motivational business presentation	Design presentation to include short message from president, pictures of company product line, graphs of projected sales, sound effects of cheering crowds, brief video demo of new product
Entertainment	Animate adventure game	Control the instrument panel of a spacecraft, discuss tactics with crew members on screen, hear sounds of engines, real-time map displays
Education	Learn a foreign language	Watch and listen to a short language video segment and view a synchronized translation

FIGURE 2-11: *A multimedia PC*

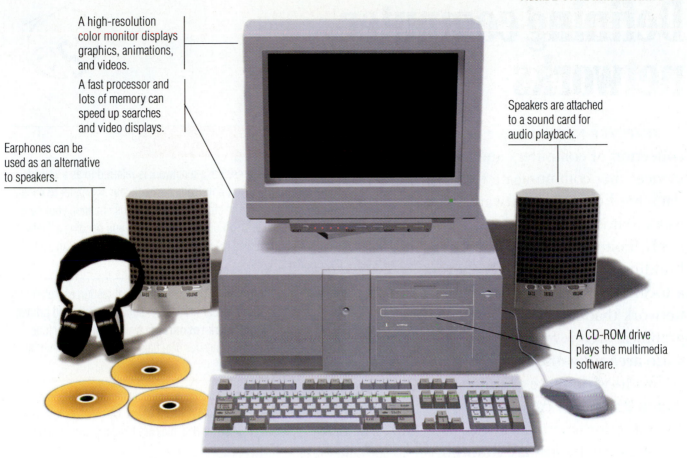

A high-resolution color monitor displays graphics, animations, and videos.

A fast processor and lots of memory can speed up searches and video displays.

Earphones can be used as an alternative to speakers.

Speakers are attached to a sound card for audio playback.

A CD-ROM drive plays the multimedia software.

FIGURE 2-12: *A hypertext of linked documents*

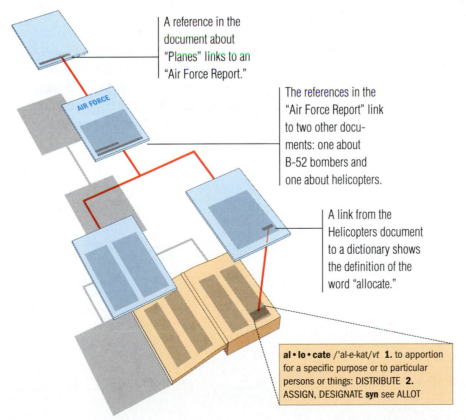

A reference in the document about "Planes" links to an "Air Force Report."

The references in the "Air Force Report" link to two other documents: one about B-52 bombers and one about helicopters.

A link from the Helicopters document to a dictionary shows the definition of the word "allocate."

al • lo • cate /ˈal-e-kat/ *vt* **1.** to apportion for a specific purpose or to particular persons or things: DISTRIBUTE **2.** ASSIGN, DESIGNATE **syn** see ALLOT

QUICK TIP

If you already have a computer, but it is not equipped for multimedia, you can add multimedia capabilities by purchasing a multimedia kit that contains a CD-ROM drive and sound card.

FYI

Most multimedia applications are shipped on a CD-ROM because the graphics, sound, and video require large amounts of storage space. However, not everything shipped on CD-ROM is multimedia. Many software publishers distribute large data files and non-multimedia software on CD-ROM because one CD-ROM is more convenient and more cost effective than twenty or thirty floppy disks.

Defining computer networks

A **COMPUTER NETWORK** IS A collection of computers and other devices that communicate to share data, hardware, and software. A network that is located within a relatively limited area such as a building or campus is referred to as a **local area network** or **LAN**. A network that covers a large geographical area is referred to as a **wide area network** or **WAN**.

World-wide there are an estimated 25 million computers connected to local area networks. Local area networks are found in most medium and large businesses, government offices, and educational institutions. Not all LANs are the same. Different types of networks provide different services, use different technology, have different resources, and require users to follow different procedures.

IN MORE DETAIL

- A computer that is not connected to a network is referred to as a **stand-alone computer**. When you physically connect your computer to a local area network, using a cable or other communications channel, your computer becomes a **workstation** on the network and you become a "network user." Figure 2-13 illustrates the workstations, network server, and other network resources.

- Network resources: Your workstation has all its usual resources, referred to as **local resources**, such as your hard drive, software, data, and printer. You also have access to **network resources**, which typically include application software, storage space for data files, and printers other than those on your local workstation.

- A **network server** is a computer that is connected to the network and that "serves," or distributes resources to network users. On a network, application software and storage space for data files are typically provided by a network server.

- A **network printer** provides output capabilities to all the network users.

- Each device on a network, including workstations, servers, and printers, is referred to as a **node**.

- Sharing resources: The main advantage of a computer network is that all the users can share resources, instead of users each maintaining their own. For example, a LAN permits many users to share a single printer. Most organizations with LANs are able to reduce the overall number of printers needed, reduce printer maintenance costs, and use the money saved to buy higher quality printers.

FIGURE 2-13: *Local and network resources*

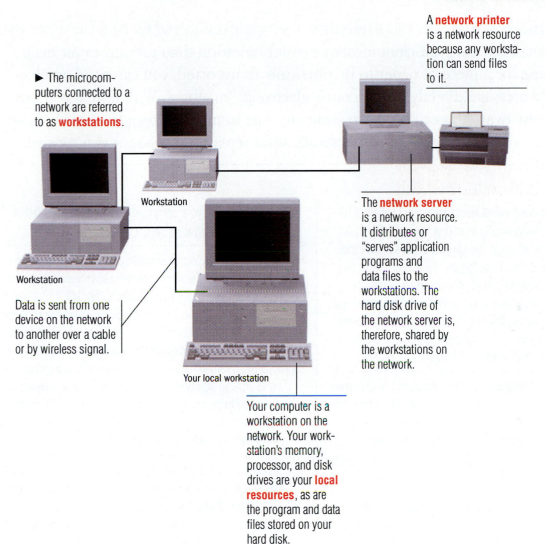

A **network printer** is a network resource because any workstation can send files to it.

▶ The microcomputers connected to a network are referred to as **workstations**.

Workstation

Workstation

Data is sent from one device on the network to another over a cable or by wireless signal.

Your local workstation

The **network server** is a network resource. It distributes or "serves" application programs and data files to the workstations. The hard disk drive of the network server is, therefore, shared by the workstations on the network.

Your computer is a workstation on the network. Your workstation's memory, processor, and disk drives are your **local resources**, as are the program and data files stored on your hard disk.

QUICK TIP

Most users and technical support people refer to local area networks simply as "networks."

Exploring electronic mail (e-mail)

ELECTRONIC MAIL, OR E-MAIL, IS CORRESPONDENCE CONDUCTED BETWEEN ONE OR MORE USERS on a network. E-mail is a more efficient means of communication than ground or air mail. Rather than waiting for a piece of paper to be physically transported, you can send an electronic version of a message directly to someone's electronic "mailbox." With e-mail you can send messages right away. You can send the same message to multiple people as easily as sending to a single person, and it is easy to automatically send replies to messages you receive.

IN MORE DETAIL

- **How e-mail works:** An **e-mail message** is essentially a letter or memo sent electronically from one user to another. An **electronic mail system** is the hardware and software that collects and delivers e-mail messages. Typically, a local area network provides electronic mail services to its users. The software on the network server that controls the flow of e-mail is called **mail server software**. The software on a workstation that helps each user read, compose, send, and delete messages is called **mail client software**.

- **Store and forward technology:** E-mail messages are *stored* on a server. When you want to read this mail, the server *forwards* the messages to your workstation. Hence e-mail is called a **store and forward technology**. Because the server stores the messages, your workstation does not need to be on when someone sends you e-mail.

- **Getting your mail:** When someone sends you e-mail, the message is stored on a host or network server in an area you can think of as your **mailbox**. Refer to figure 2-14. When you log into the electronic mail system and check your mail, the message is listed as new mail. You can choose to display and read the mail on your computer screen, print it, delete it, reply to it, forward it, or save it on disk.

- **Features:** Some electronic mail systems offer features such as **priority mail**, which immediately alerts the recipient that an e-mail message has arrived; **return receipt**, which sends a message back to you when a recipient receives your message; **carbon copy**, which sends a copy of the message to another user; and **group addressing**, which allows you to send a copy of an e-mail message to all members of a group at the same time. In addition to these features, some e-mail systems allow you to send an **attachment**, which is a file such as a word processing document, worksheet, or graphic that travels along with an electronic mail message.

- **Sending e-mail out of network:** What if you want to send e-mail to someone who is not connected to your computer network or host? Many e-mail systems are connected to other e-mail systems through electronic links called **gateways**. When you send an e-mail message to a user on another computer network, the message is transferred through the gateway to a larger e-mail system, which delivers the message to the recipient's network or host computer system.

E-mail privacy

You should be aware that your e-mail might be read by someone other than the recipient. Although the U.S. justice system has not yet made a clear ruling, current legal interpretations indicate that e-mail is not legally protected from snooping. You cannot assume that the e-mail you send is private.

Therefore, you should not use e-mail to send any message that you want to keep confidential. Some employers read employee e-mail to discover if any illegal activities are taking place on the computer system. Many employers are genuinely concerned about such activities because they could, in some cases, be held responsible for the actions of their employees. Also, it sometimes happens that the network administrator sees the contents of e-mail messages while performing system maintenance or when trying to recover from a system failure.

FIGURE 2-14: *Using e-mail*

The Lotus Notes software handles each user's personal mail box.

Icons and tools help you easily read mail, send mail and replies.

The Lotus Notes window shows you a list of messages; the time they were sent, the sender's name, and the subject of each message.

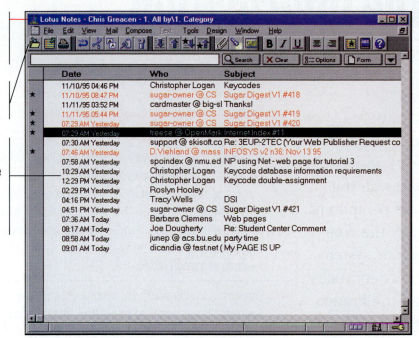

The advantages of e-mail can also create potential problems. Refer to Table 2-2 for some tips to help you avoid e-mail problems.

TABLE 2-2: *Tips to help you avoid e-mail problems*

TIP	WHY IT'S IMPORTANT
Read your mail regularly	When you use electronic mail, your correspondents expect a quick response
Delete messages after you read them	Your e-mail is stored, along with everyone else's on a file server where storage space is valuable; leaving old messages in your mailbox takes up space that could be used more productively
Don't reply to every e-mail message	The purpose of some e-mail messages is to give you information; don't reply unless there is a reason to respond, such as to answer a question
If you receive mail addressed to a group, it might be better to reply only to one person in the group	You might receive mail as a member of a mailing list; the same message will be sent to everyone on the list. If you use the automatic reply feature of your e-mail system, your message is likely to be sent to everyone on the list.
Think before you send	It is easy to write a message in haste or in anger and send it off before you have time to think it through; if you're upset, write your message, but wait a day before you send it
Don't write anything you want to remain confidential	Remember that with electronic mail it is easy to forward messages
Don't get sloppy	Your e-mail is a reflection of you, your school, and your employer. Use a spell-checker if one is available; if not, proofread your message before you send it. Use standard grammar, punctuation, and capitalization. A message in all uppercase means you're shouting.

Touring the information highway

THE **INFORMATION HIGHWAY** IS A world-wide network of computers linked by telephone lines and satellites. The "towns" or **sites** on the information highway are computers. The "roads" that connect the computers are communications systems provided by common carriers such as AT&T, and MCI, and the French telephone company, Minitel. The "cars" that travel along the information highway carry information of all kinds. If someone were to draw a simplified diagram or "map" of the information highway it might look like Figure 2-15.

You can access the information on this highway using a microcomputer and a communications link. That link must be established through a modem which is part of your computer system or the network system. The information highway includes a huge computer network called the Internet.

FIGURE 2-15: *Commercial information services + the Internet = the information highway*

Millions of home computers

Hundreds of users

Small information service

Large commercial information service

Internet host computer

Internet host computer

I-way Rte I

Computer lab network

Internet host computer

I-way Rte I

University host computer

Neighborhood bulletin board service

Hundreds of home computers

KEY

■ Internet host computer

— Internet

— Commerical service

— Other service

The term "on-line service" has two meanings. It can be a synonym for a commercial information service, or it can refer to a service, such as e-mail, provided on-line.

To use the Internet, you must have an account on a network that is connected to the Internet, and your network administrator must approve your account for Internet use. If your university network is connected to the Internet, it is likely that you have access to the Internet from the computers in your labs.

TABLE 2-3: *Information highway terms*

TERM	DEFINITION
Cyberspace	A computer-generated mental image of a computer world; the term cyberspace was coined in 1984 by science fiction writer William Gibson
Discussion group	An on-line forum for discussing issues with a group of people
Download	Electronically transporting a file from a host computer to a local computer
Chat session	Many people participating in an on-line discussion by simply typing their comments

Understanding how the Internet works

THE INTERNET IS ESSENTIALLY A network of networks. Although each of the smaller networks connected to the Internet is owned by an individual, a corporation, an educational institution, or a government agency, no one "owns" the Internet.

With over 20,000 of these networks, it is currently impossible for each computer to have a direct link to every network on the Internet. Information cannot be sent directly from one network to its final destination. Instead, information is handed from one network to another until it reaches its destination.

IN MORE DETAIL

o-π Internet services: The Internet offers e-mail, discussion groups, government documents, computer technical support, on-line shopping, interactive entertainment, downloadable software, music, graphics, and video clips. On the Internet, there are thousands of discussion groups and millions of documents.

o-π Internet access: Many different software packages are available to help you access different types of Internet information and services. The trend today is to use a single software package to access most Internet services.

o-π Internet addresses: On the Internet, people and computers are identified by addresses. Every computer on the Internet has an address made up of four groups of numbers, for example, 172.201.25.1. Because it is difficult to remember long strings of numbers, numerical addresses are converted into names such as "jsc.nasa.gov."

People with accounts on Internet computers are identified by addresses such as **president@whitehouse.gov**. This Internet address means the following: The first part of the address, *president*, is the **user ID**—in this case the user ID is for the President of the United States. The **@ sign** separates the user ID from the machine name. A **machine name** is the unique set of numbers and letters that identifies each computer connected to the Internet. In the example, the machine name is "whitehouse," a computer in Washington D.C. that handles the White House Internet connection. A period separates the machine name from the domain name. The **domain name** groups the computers on the Internet into the following categories: com (commercial), edu (educational), gov (nonmilitary government), mil (military), org (other organizations), or net (network resources). In the address president@whitehouse.gov, the domain is gov, indicating that the whitehouse computer is maintained by a non-military agency of the government.

o-π Internet e-mail: When you send e-mail via the Internet, your local mail server software examines the machine name in the address of each message. The mail is delivered to computers at those Internet addresses. Figure 2-15 shows how the Internet routes e-mail from a student at the University of Alaska to a student at the University of the Virgin Islands.

FIGURE 2-15: *Internet e-mail routes*

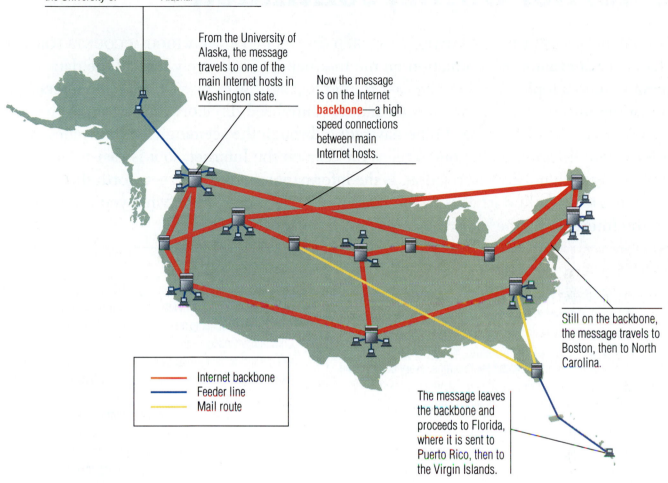

The message origi- nates from a computer in a student's apart- ment one block from the University of

Alaska campus. The message travels over the telephone lines to the University of Alaska.

From the University of Alaska, the message travels to one of the main Internet hosts in Washington state.

Now the message is on the Internet **backbone**—a high speed connections between main Internet hosts.

Still on the backbone, the message travels to Boston, then to North Carolina.

The message leaves the backbone and proceeds to Florida, where it is sent to Puerto Rico, then to the Virgin Islands.

— Internet backbone
— Feeder line
— Mail route

The history of the Internet

The history of the Internet begins in 1957 when the Soviet Union launched Sputnik, the first artificial satellite. In response to this display of Soviet technical expertise, the U.S. government resolved to improve its science and techni- cal infrastructure. One of the resulting initiatives was the Advanced Research Projects Agency (ARPA), created by the Department of Defense. The plan was to construct a network of geographically dispersed computers that would continue to function even if one of the computers on the network was destroyed. In 1969 four com- puter networks were connected to each other and called ARPANET. Connecting two or more networks creates an **internetwork** or **internet**, so ARPANET was one of the first examples of an internet (with a lower case i). Gradually, more and more networks were con- nected to the ARPANET, and it became known as the Internet (with an uppercase I).

Understanding how the Internet works, continued

NO ONE DECIDES WHERE INFORMATION IS STORED ON THE INTERNET, WHICH ACCOUNTS FOR THE chaotic organization of information on the Internet. You will rarely find all the data pertaining to a topic stored in one easy to find location. With over 20,000 computers providing information on the Internet and no centralized directory of services, even experienced users have a hard time navigating through the seemingly endless miles of information. In addition, no one screens the data on the Internet, so it is easy to get junk along with quality information. Is the information on the Internet worth the trouble it takes to find it? This lesson continues by briefing you on what you can find on the Internet and the tools you can use to facilitate your search.

IN MORE DETAIL

○━ The World Wide Web: Currently, some of the best organized and most accessible information on the Internet is available through a service called the **World Wide Web**, abbreviated **WWW**, but often referred to simply as "the Web." The information available on the Web covers almost every conceivable topic and the information is often presented in a multimedia format with graphics, music, or video clips.

○━ Web pages: The official description of the World Wide Web is a "wide-area hypermedia information retrieval initiative aiming to give universal access to a large universe of documents." The World Wide Web consists of pages, called **web pages**, each of which contains information on a particular topic.

○━ Web links: In addition to topic information, a web page might also include one or more links to other web pages. **Links** are pointers to other web pages that make it easy to follow a thread of related information, even if the pages are stored on computers located in different continents. Figure 2-16 shows a conceptual model of how the World Wide Web works.

○━ HTML: To offer World Wide Web service, an Internet site must set up web server software and format its information into pages using a Hypertext Markup Language (HTML) editor. An **HTML editor** creates links between pages, displays links in boldface underlined text, and positions graphics.

○━ Each web page has a unique address called a **uniform resource locator (URL)**. To access a web page, you must either follow a link or type a URL. You can find listings of web page URLs in books, such as *Walking the World Wide Web*,

and in Internet magazines such as *Wired*. You can also access an on-line directory of Web pages using URLs specific

A **URL** is similar to an e-mail address. For example, Honolulu Community College is the Web site for a dinosaur exhibit. The URL for this exhibit is http://www.hcc.hawaii.edu/dinos.1.html. And that's just a short URL! Let's look at each part of the URL to see what it means.

http:// WWW documents are sent between sites using HyperText Transfer Protocol (HTTP). The *http://* at the beginning of the dinosaur URL indicates that this is a WWW page. Whenever you see a long string of characters that begins with http://, you know it is referring to a WWW page.

www.hcc.hawaii.edu Some elements of this URL might look familiar—www.*hcc.hawaii.edu* is the Internet address for the World Wide Web server at Honolulu Community College. Many Web server addresses begin with *www*. The *.edu* indicates this is a site maintained by an educational institution.

/dinos.1.html. The last part of the URL, */dinos.1.html*, refers specifically to the dinosaur WWW page. Honolulu Community College might have other WWW pages, such as *dinos.2.html* and *dinos.3.html*. This last part of the URL differentiates among the pages at a particular site.

○━ Web browsers: To access World Wide Web information, you need a computer with Internet access and software called a **web browser**. A web browser displays the text, graphics, and links for a web page. It also helps you follow the links from one document to another. Web browser software packages include Netscape, Mosaic, Lynx, and Cello. Figure 2-17 shows you how to use a web browser to access information on the World Wide Web.

FIGURE 2-16: *How the World Wide Web works*

Honolulu Community College (HCC) maintains an exhibit containing images, video clips, narration, and text about dinosaurs. Each image, video, and document is a separate **page**, stored as a file on the HCC computer. You can jump from one page to another at HCC. For example, you can begin at the introductory screen, called a **home page**.

From the home page, you can jump to a page about iguanas.

From this page you can jump to a page that contains a movie.

HCC also has links to other web sites with dinosaur information. You can jump to one of these sites by clicking the underlined text.

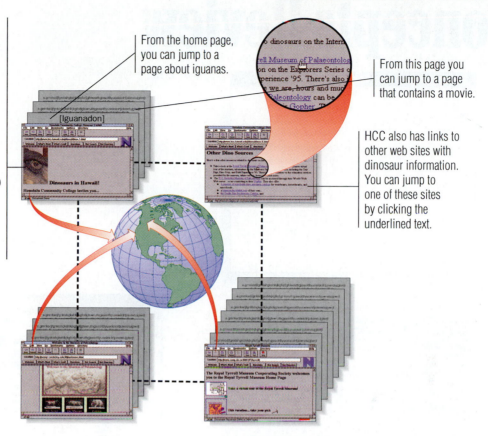

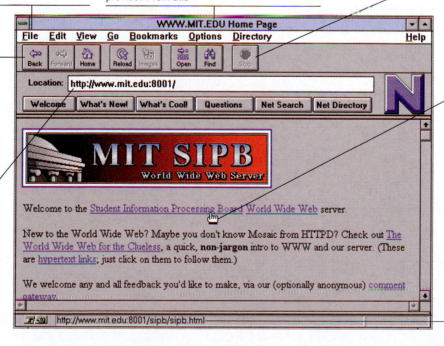

FIGURE 2-17: *Using Netscape Navigator software*

You can use the File menu to print out pages or save them on your local hard disk drive.

When you start the web browser, it displays the home page of our Internet service provider. From this page you jump to other Web pages anywhere on the World Wide Web.

The Stop button halts the transfer of a page. Sometimes the pages are very large and you don't want to wait for them.

The Back button helps you navigate to pages you have previously viewed. The Next button shows you the next page in the sequence.

If you know the URL of the page to which you want to jump, you can type the URL in the box. All World Wide Web URLs begin with **http://**.

You can jump to linked documents by clicking any of the underlined text. On most web browsers, the pointer changes to a hand when it is positioned over a text or graphical link.

The status bar keeps you updated. Here the status bar shows that the pointer is positioned on a link to Student Information Processing located at **http://www.mit.edu. 8001/sipb/sipb.html.** If you select this link, the status bar shows how long it will take for the page to be transmitted.

Concepts Review

FIGURE 2-18

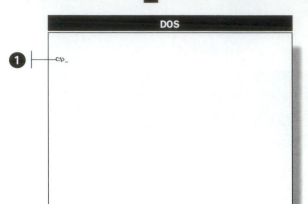

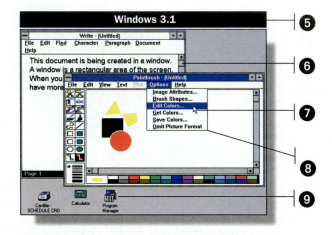

Label each element shown in Figure 2-18.

1. _____

2. _____

3. _____

4. _____

5. _____

6. _____

7. _____

8. _____

9. _____

Match each statement with the term it describes.

10. ____ Software

11. ____ Windows

12. ____ CD-ROM

15. ____ magnetic storage

16. ____ optical storage

17. ____ data

18. ____ .txt

19. ____ local area network (LAN)

20. ____ network server

21. ____ node

a. each device on a network, including workstations, servers, and printers

b. Operating system for an IBM computer

c. computer connected to the network that "serves," or distributes resources to network users

d. data burned into medium with laser light

e. filename extension for general category of text file

f. Stores multimedia software

g. words, numbers, and graphics

h. Instructions and associated data stored in electronic format

i. network that is located within a relatively limited area

j. magnetized particles of oxidized-based surface coating

Fill in the best answer.

22. When you type a report or enter the information for a mailing list, you are creating _____.

23. The instructions that tell a computer how to convert inches to centimeters are a computer _____.

24. _____ software helps the *computer* carry out its basic operating tasks.

25. Multimedia applications combine media such as _____, _____, _____, _____, _____, and _____.

26. You can add multimedia capability to your computer by purchasing a(n) _____ _____ designed to be installed in a few hours by a non-technical user.

27. If you want to run more than one program at a time, you must use an operating system with _____ capability.

28. To differentiate between data and information, use the rule: _____ is used by computers; _____ is used by humans.

29. Nested file folders and directory trees are ways of representing _____ storage.

30. Storage capacity is measured in _____.

31. A magnet can disrupt data on _____ storage, but _____ storage technology is more durable.

32. The primary storage device on a microcomputer is _____.

33. The _____ keeps track of the physical location of files on a disk.

34. Data files which are entered by the user, changed often, or shared with other users are generally stored on _____ media.

35. A network _____ is a computer connected to a network that distributes files to network users.

36. A(n) _____ is devoted to the task of delivering program and data files to workstations.

37. Three reasons why sharing programs is effective for an organization are _____, _____, and _____.

38. The _____ is a collection of local, regional, and national computer networks that are linked together to exchange data and distribute processing tasks.

39. A(n) _____ charges its subscribers a fee to access information.

40. A(n) _____ is an on-line discussion in which participants post a question or comment, then log in later after other participants have had a chance to respond.

41. The process of transferring files containing text, graphics, music, or video clips from a remote computer to your computer is called _____.

42. Most commercial information services have a(n) _____ that covers services such as electronic mail, current news, games, discussion groups, and on-line shopping.

43. When you connect two or more networks, you form a(n) _____.

44. The _____ is the largest and most widely used network in the world.

45. Identify each part of the Internet address: coco@canine.com.

46. Which Internet service would you use to access the URL http://physics7.berkeley.edu/home.html?

INDEPENDENT CHALLENGE 1

In this unit you learned how to identify microcomputer operating systems by looking at the main screen and prompt. In this independent challenge you will explore more about the operating system in your school computer lab. If you have more than one lab or your computer uses more than one operating system, your instructor should tell you which one to use for the independent challenge.

To complete this independent challenge:

1. Find out which operating system is used in your school computer lab. Be sure you find out the type and version. You can obtain this information on-line from one of the computers. If you see a command-line user interface, try typing "ver" and then pressing the Enter key. If you see a graphical user interface, try clicking the Apple menu or click the Help menu, then select Help About.

2. Once you know the operating system used in your school lab, use the operating system reference manual and library resources to answer the following questions:

   a. Which operating system and version is used in your school lab?

   b. What company publishes the operating system software?

   c. When was the first version of this operating system introduced?

   d. Does this operating system have a command-line user interface or a graphical user interface?

   e. Does this operating system support multi-tasking?

   f. Do you need a password to use the computers in your school lab? Even if you do not need to use a password, does the operating system provide some way to secure access to the computers?

   g. How much does the publisher of this operating system usually charge for upgrades if you are a registered user?

INDEPENDENT CHALLENGE 2

You learned in this unit that most users do not need to write programs in order to use their computers. But you also learned that computer programming is a challenging career field. In this independent challenge you will find out more about computer programming careers.

Computer programming jobs are often listed on the back pages of computer magazines, in professional journals, and on career bulletin boards on the Internet. Some of the best sources of information are:

Infoworld magazine
The professional journal Communications of the ACM
The newspaper San Jose Mercury News and its Internet site http://www.sjmercury.com
The Internet Monster Board http://www.monster.com
The Internet Career Mosaic http://www.careermosaic.com
The Internet site http://rescomp.stanford.edu has a list of other Internet job listings

To complete this independent challenge:

1. Locate three advertisements for computer programming jobs. Photocopy or get a computer printout of the ads. Create a table like the one that follows and fill it in for each of the three job openings you found.

	Job 1	Job 2	Job 3
Educational requirements			
Work experience required			
Programming languages required			
Mainframe, mini, or microcomputer			
Company name			
Starting salary			

There are so many software packages that it is difficult to get an idea of what's available unless you take a look through current computer magazines and software catalogs. This Independent Challenge has two parts. You can do either one or both as your instructor assigns. Part 1 helps you discover the breadth of available software applications. Part 2 helps you research an application or operating system in more depth. You will be able to find the information for this independent challenge in computer magazines in your library. If you have access to the Internet, check out Computer Express at http://www.cexpress.com:2700.

To complete this independent challenge:

1. Find an ad for a computer vendor that sells a large variety of software. Jot down the name of the vendor and where you found the ad. List the categories the vendor uses to classify software and the number of software packages in each category.

2. Select one type of software from the following categories: operating systems, disk utilities, word processing, graphics, presentation graphics, electronic mail, desktop publishers, spreadsheets, database, accounting, or scheduling. Read a comparison review of software packages in the category you select. Next try to locate and photocopy ads for each of the products in the review. Look through the software vendor ads to find the best price for each product. Finally, write a one- or two-page summary explaining your purchase recommendation.

Many software applications use a specific file extension for data files created with that application. Determine the extensions used by five applications on your own or a lab computer.

To complete this independent challenge:

1. Run each software application and attempt to retrieve a file. If the software application uses a specific file extension, you will usually see the extension indicated in a box on the screen. For example, you might see *.DOC if you are using Microsoft Word for Windows.

2. For each of the five programs you select, specify the program name, sketch a picture of the program icon (if you are using Windows), indicate the executable filename (if you are using DOS), and indicate the filename extension the program uses. If the program does not use a specific filename extension, indicate that this is the case.

Appendix:
A Buyer's Guide

WHETHER YOU ARE A FIRST TIME BUYER OR upgrading, when the time comes to make your computer buying decision, you may find yourself overwhelmed by the information available to you. There are thousands of computer advertisements in magazines and newspapers featuring lists of technical specifications. To get the best deal on the computer that meets your specific needs, you need to understand what these technical specifications mean and how they will affect your computing power. This Buyer's Guide consists of seven lessons to help you organize and make your purchasing decisions. This simple guide can help organize your thoughts during the decision-making process.

OBJECTIVES

Basic computer system

Computer architecture

Systems and applications software and storage

Special considerations for notebook computers

Peripheral devices

Multimedia computing

Service and support agreements

Basic computer system

THE FIRST DECISION YOU WILL MAKE IS determining the basic configuration for your new computer system.

The *Computer Shopper* is a periodical that has hundreds of advertisements from national resellers. It will give you a broad base of vendors from which to choose and compare features and prices to help you purchase a computer.

First, establish the budget for your computer system. Many system configurations will be excluded from your choices as being too costly; this helps your decision-making by limiting your options.

Computer architecture

BUYER'S GUIDE

ONCE YOU HAVE ESTABLISHED THE basic configuration of your computer system, you need to think about the computer architecture. These technical specifications will ultimately determine your computing power.

☞ **Network or stand-alone?** Are you going to be working as part of a network or alone? Do you plan to tie into a network and take advantage of a central file server and microprocessor using your computer as a workstation?

☞ **Which microprocessor?** Compare microprocessors to determine the best one within the platform. Whether you choose the Motorola 68000-series (for the Macintosh), PowerPC (for PC or Macintosh), or Intel x86 families (for IBM compatibles).

☞ **What clock speed?** Processors come in various speeds that affect the performance of processing. If you plan to use your computer for complex scientific, mathematical, or graphics applications you probably want to get a faster computer than if you're simply using it for word processing.

☞ **How much RAM?** The amount of RAM a computer needs depends on the operating system and the applications you plan to run. The minimum recommended RAM for today's computing is 8MB (megabytes) although many applications can require up to 16MB. It is possible to add RAM at the cost of about $50 per megabyte after you purchase your system.

☞ **Include RAM cache?** A RAM cache is very important to optimum performance of computers with high-speed processors because the CPU can process data faster than it can retrieve it from the regular RAM area. A computer with an 80486 microprocessor should have at least 128K of RAM cache; a Pentium system should have at least 256K.

☞ **Bus and slot types** Computer ads generally specify the type of expansion bus the computer uses to transport data. The capacity of the expansion bus is determined by its speed, measured in megahertz (MHZ), and the number of bits that can be transported during each clock cycle.

Systems and applications software and storage

BUYER'S GUIDE

WHAT WILL YOU BE USING YOUR computer for? Although you can build your software library over time, the operating system you choose determines what software will be available to you. You must also consider how your system will store these programs.

Operating system. The platform you choose (Macintosh or IBM-compatible) will drive your choices of operating system. Vendors typically include the operating system with the computer, so if you purchase an IBM-compatible computer, you can expect that the latest version of DOS and Windows will be preinstalled on the hard drive. You may choose to purchase and switch operating systems at a later time.

Software bundles. Many vendors also include applications software such as a word processor or basic games with a computer system. Multimedia computer systems usually include several CD-ROMs, such as encyclopedias, fact books, and games. All other factors being equal, a system with bundled software will cost slightly more than a system without bundled software. However, if the software meets your needs, the slight increase in price is generally less than you would pay if you bought the software separately.

Hard disk. Hard disks are defined by their storage capacity which is measured in kilobytes, megabytes, or gigabytes. The larger (more bytes) the hard disk can store, the more data and programs can be stored on your computer system. As storage technology continues to become less expensive, hard disks with greater than 1.0 gigabytes are becoming very common.

Floppy drives. Typically, floppy disks are the storage medium you will use to transfer and save data. Since the 5.25" floppy is rapidly becoming obsolete (going the way of the 8" floppy) a single 3.5" floppy drive should meet your needs.

Special considerations for notebook computers

IF YOU DECIDE TO BUY A NOTEBOOK COMPUTER, THERE ARE ADDITIONAL DECISIONS YOU must make. Special considerations apply to the source of power, parts, and input and output devices.

LCD display. Notebook computers do not use monitors because they are too big and require too much power to run on batteries. Instead, notebooks have a flat panel liquid crystal display. A liquid crystal display (LCD) can either be passive or active matrix. Passive matrix screens rely on timing to update the display update; as a result, moving images can appear blurred. Active matrix screens update more rapidly and provide image quality similar to that of a monitor. Passive matrix screens, the least expensive, are available in monochrome or color, which are more expensive. Color active matrix screens are necessary for a crisp display of graphics, animation, and video and are the most expensive.

VGA port. Most notebook computers have a VGA port for an external monitor. This port gives you the option of using a monitor, if available, with your notebook computer.

PCMCIA slot. The PCMCIA slots a special type of expansion slot developed for use with notebook computers that allows you to insert a PCMCIA card. PCMCIA slots are categorized by size; Type I (the thinnest, used mostly for expansion memory cards), Type II (the most popular, accepts cards that contain modems, sound cards, or network cards), or Type III (the thickest which contain devices such as hard disk drives.) Many notebooks provide a multipurpose PCMCIA slot that will accept two Type I cards, two Type II cards, or one Type III card.

Weight. Notebook computers can weigh as little as 4 pounds or as much as 10 pounds or more. Consider how much you will be carrying your computer around to determine if weight is a factor.

Power source. Notebook computers operate on power from both batteries and a wall outlet. The choice depends on your location adding to their portability.

Battery types include nickle-metal-hydride and a newer lithium battery which has a better recharging capacity. Some notebooks also have the option to replace a drive with a second battery to extend the usable time away from a wall outlet or recharge.

Mouse type. Although a mouse is the standard pointing device for desktop computers, alternative pointing devices such as built-in track ball, track point, and touch pad are more convenient to use with notebook computers.

Docking bay. In order to provide multimedia computing in the small carrying case of a notebook, alternative devices such as docking bays and port extenders have been developed. A docking bay is essentially an additional expansion bus into which you plug your notebook. The notebook provides the processor and RAM, the docking bay provides expansion ports for additional devices such as a sound card and CD-ROM drive.

Case to carry. Consider how you will carry your notebook computer and purchase a case that is well designed. The case should be well padded to protect the computer as well as provide the necessary compartments to store extra devices, power cords and cables, and any papers or notes you may carry.

Peripheral devices

PERIPHERAL DEVICES ADD FUNCTIONALITY TO YOUR COMPUTER SYSTEM BY GIVING YOU different options for input, output, and storage. If budget is limited, you do not have to include all of these devices when you buy your computer system. You can add any of them to your computer system as your needs and budget permit.

IN MORE DETAIL

Pointing device. The computer mouse is the standard pointing device for desktop computers. There are several types to choose from. The serial mouse connects to your serial port, the bus mouse connects directly to a bus port, if available on the motherboard or peripheral card. Also available is an infrared mouse which does not connect to your computer with a cable. Infrared is used to transmit the movements and clicks to a receiver that plugs into the port on your computer.

Printer. Printers are characterized as dot matrix, ink jet, or laser. Color printers are available in each category but color ink-jet printers offer the best price-performance because of the high price of color laser printers and the poor quality of color dot-matrix printers.

Scanner. A scanner reads images from a page and converts it to digital representation. It is a fast way to convert images on paper to data that can be manipulated. Depending on the software you purchase with your scanner you can use scanners to enter character data.

Modem. Many computer systems include a modem that transmits and receives data over phone lines to other computers. Baud rate identifies the transmission speed. Faster baud rates mean faster transmission; new systems should come with a minimum 14,400 ("14 dot 4") modem but are better served with a 28.8 baud modem

Fax modems. A fax modem is a modem that includes fax capability. This means that it can send a document that is in the memory of your computer to any standard fax machine, where it appears in hard copy format, or other fax modem to be printed later. Fax modems can also receive fax transmissions from standard fax machines or other fax modems.

Backup system. Depending on how much and how often you want to backup the data from your hard disk you may consider adding a tape backup system to your computer.

Surge protector. A surge protector protects your computer system against sudden fluctuations in power.

Game port/joy stick. If you are planning to use your computer to play games that require motion input, you will need to purchase a computer system with a game port as well as the joy stick or flight yoke, depending on your application.

Multimedia computing

To take advantage of the latest features of today's software including images, sound, and video you should consider adding multimedia capabilities to your computer system. If your budget is limited but you still want access to the text and reference software distributed on CD-ROM, you can purchase the CD-ROM drive with your basic computer system and add the sound card and speakers later.

IN MORE DETAIL

- **CD-ROM drive.** A CD-ROM drive, either a quad-speed (4X) or six-speed (6X) is a worthwhile investment that lets you use multimedia, game, educational and reference applications that are only available on CD-ROM. Eight-speed (8X) are now becoming available for the fastest data retrieval.

- **Sound card / speakers.** Most games and multimedia applications require a sound card and speakers. A sound card adds only $100 or so to the price of a computer system and most users would say that it is worth the price for the capability to run multimedia applications.

Service and support agreements

AS WITH ANY MAJOR PURCHASE, THE level of service and support provided by the vendor or manufacturer should be a major consideration in your buying decision.

IN MORE DETAIL

Guarantee. Computer systems are major investments. Does the manufacturer provide reasonable guarantees on the equipment? Does the manufacturer or the vendor guarantee the system? Do you get a labor and parts warranty? Consider the reputation of the manufacturer and the service and support that will be made available to you.

Telephone support. If you have a problem and need to call the manufacturer or vendor, do they have a local or toll-free number? What is the typical waiting time for a technical support person?

Local repair. If you need a component repaired, will the system be repaired locally? Do you have to send it out? Who pays shipping? Do you get a replacement while you wait for the system or part to be repaired? Some manufacturers have an instant exchange program for components giving you a refurbished unit in exchange for yours.

Glossary

.ZIP ▶ The file extension of files created with PKZIP, a popular data compression utility. Sometimes called "zipped" files.

Alt key ▶ The key used in combination with other keys to produce different results depending on the software you are using.

Application software ▶ Software that helps the human user carry out a task.

Attachment ▶ A file such as a word processing document, worksheet, or graphic that travels through the e-mail system along with an electronic mail message.

Backspace key ▶ The key that deletes the character to the left of the cursor.

Bar code reader ▶ Gathers input data by reading bar codes, such as the universal product codes on supermarket products.

Bit-map display ▶ (graphics display) A type of display that divides the screen into a matrix of small dots, or pixels.

Button ▶ Helps you to make a selection when using a program.

Byte ▶ How data is stored—a series of eight bits that usually represent one character.

Caps Lock key ▶ A toggle key that capitalizes all the letters you type when it is engaged, but does not produce the top symbol on keys that contain two symbols.

Carbon copy ▶ A feature offered by some electronic mail systems which sends a copy of the message to another user.

CD-ROM ▶ (pronounced "cee dee rom") Stands for Compact Disc Read Only Memory. A computer CD-ROM disk, like its audio counterpart, contains data that has been stamped on the disk surface as a series of pits.

Central Processing Unit (CPU) ▶ The circuitry in a computer that performs arithmetic and logic operations and executes instructions.

Character-based display ▶ A type of display that divides the screen into a grid of rectangles, which can each display a single character.

Chat session ▶ Many people participating in an on-line discussion by simply typing their comments.

Click ▶ To press the left mouse button a single time to select an object on the monitor.

Cluster ▶ A group of sectors, the smallest storage unit the computer can access.

Command ▶ An instruction you input to tell the computer to carry out a task.

Command-line user interface ▶ An interface that requires the user to type in commands.

Commercial information service ▶ A service that provides access to computer-based information and services for a fee. Also called an online service.

Compatible ▶ Computers that operate in essentially the same way.

Computer ▶ A device that accepts input, processes data, stores data, and produces output.

Computer bulletin board service ▶ A computerized information exchange that is accessible with a modem. Also referred to as a BBS.

Computer program ▶ A set of instructions which tells the computer how to perform a particular task.

Computer projector ▶ Generates a large image of what is on the computer screen.

Computer system ▶ A computer and its hardware, peripheral devices, and software.

Control unit ▶ The part of the Central Processing Unit that directs and coordinates processing.

Ctrl or Control key ▶ The key used in combination with other keys to produce different results depending on the software you are using.

Cursor ▶ A flashing underline on the screen, indicates where the characters you type will appear.

Cursor keys ▶ Move your position on the screen up, down, right, or left.

Cyberspace ▶ A computer-generated mental image of a computer world. Coined in 1984 by science fiction writer William Gibson.

Data ▶ Refers to the words, numbers, and graphics that describe people, events, things, and ideas. A computer processes data.

Data compression ▶ A technique that reduces the size of a large file by using fewer bits to represent the data that the file contains on the disk.

Data files ▶ A file that contains words, numbers, and pictures that you can view, edit, save, send, and print.

Defragmentation utility ▶ A computer function used to rearrange the files on a disk so that they are stored in adjacent clusters.

Desktop metaphor ▶ A metaphor using documents as file folders and storage as a filing cabinet.

Dialog box ▶ A box that displays the options associated with a command.

Discussion group ▶ An on-line forum for discussing issues with a group of people.

Domain name ▶ A designation at the end of an address that groups the computers on the Internet into the following categories: com (commercial), edu (educational), gov (nonmilitary government), mil (military), org (other organizations), or net (network resources.)

Double-click ▶ To click the mouse twice in rapid succession.

Download ▶ Electronically transporting a file from a host computer to a local computer.

Drag ▶ To move an object from one screen location to another by selecting the object, holding down the mouse button, and moving the mouse to the new location.

Electronic mail (e-mail) ▶ Correspondence conducted between one or more users on a network.

Electronic mail software ▶ Software that provides you with a computerized mailbox that collects documents or "mail" you receive electronically from other computer users.

Electronic mail system ▶ The hardware and software that collects and delivers e-mail messages.

E-mail message ▶ Essentially a letter or memo sent electronically from one network user to another.

End key ▶ Takes you to the end of the line or the end of the document, depending on the software you are using.

Enter key ▶ Press this key when you have finished typing a command.

Error message ▶ A message conveyed by a computer if you misspell a command word, leave out required punctuation, or type the command words out of order.

Esc or Escape key ▶ Cancels an operation.

Executable file ▶ A file that contains the instructions that tell a computer how to perform a specific task.

FAT ▶ An operating system file that helps the computer store and retrieve files from disk storage by maintaining a list of files and their physical location on the disk.

File ▶ A named collection of program instructions or data that exists on a storage medium such as a hard disk, a floppy disk, or a CD-ROM.

File compression ▶ A technique that reduces the size of a large file by using fewer bits to represent the data that the file contains on the disk.

Floppy disk ▶ A flexible mylar plastic disk covered with a thin layer of magnetic oxide. Used to store data.

Floppy disk drive ▶ The storage device that records and retrieves data on a floppy disk.

Fragmented ▶ A description of files stored in many nonadjacent clusters. Decreases drive performance.

Function keys ▶ Keys on the keyboard used to initiate commands. For example, F1- F12 that execute commands such as centering a line of text or boldfacing text.

Gateways ▶ Electronic links that connect many e-mail systems.

Graphical objects ▶ Key elements of GUIs, small pictures on the screen that you can manipulate using a mouse or other input device.

Graphical user interfaces (GUIs) ▶ Pronounced "gooies", interfaces that use on-screen objects to aid the computer user.

Graphics display ▶ (bit-map display) A type of display that divides the screen into a matrix of small dots, or pixels.

Group addressing ▶ A feature offered by some electronic mail systems which allows you to send a copy of an e-mail message to all members of a group at the same time.

Hand scanner ▶ Converts a 4-6" section of text or graphics into electronic format by pulling the device over the information to be converted.

Hard disk ▶ One or more hard disk platters and their associated read-write heads.

Hardware ▶ The electric, electronic, and mechanical devices used for processing data.

Hierarchy ▶ An organization of things ranked one above the other.

Home key ▶ Takes you to the beginning of a line or the beginning of a document, depending on the software you are using.

HTML editor ▶ A hypertext markup language. Creates links between pages, displays links in boldface underlined text, and positions graphics.

Hypermedia ▶ Links that involve graphics, sound, and video, as well as text.

Hypertext ▶ A key element of many multimedia products that links documents together for easy access.

IBM-compatible computers ▶ Also referred to as PC-compatibles. Computers based on the architecture of the first IBM microcomputer.

Icon ▶ A small picture that represents an object.

Indicator lights ▶ Show you the status of each toggle key; Num Lock, Caps Lock, and Scroll Lock.

Information ▶ The words, numbers, and graphics used as the basis for human actions and decisions.

Ink jet printer ▶ A non-impact printer that ejects ink onto paper to create high-quality characters and graphics.

Input ▶ Whatever is put into a computer system.

Input device ▶ A peripheral device used to gather and translate input into a form that the computer can process.

Insertion point ▶ A flashing vertical bar on the screen, indicates where the characters you type will appear.

Internet ▶ A collection of local, regional, and national computer networks that are linked together to exchange data and distribute processing tasks.

Keyboard ▶ The primary input device for most computer systems.

LCD projection display panel ▶ Produces a large display of the information shown on a computer screen.

Links ▶ Pointers that connect one web page to other web pages.

Loading data ▶ The process of retrieving data.

Local area network (LAN) ▶ A network that is located within a relatively limited area such as a building or campus.

Local resources ▶ Devices specific to your workstation, such as your hard drive, software, data, and printer.

Logical storage ▶ A conceptual model of the way data is stored on your disk.

Machine name ▶ The unique set of numbers and letters that identifies each computer connected to the Internet. For example, "whitehouse" in the address *president@whitehouse.gov*.

Magnetic storage ▶ How a computer stores data on disks and tape. It magnetizes selected particles of an oxide-based surface coating.

Mail client software ▶ The software on a workstation that helps each user read, compose, send, and delete messages.

Mail server software ▶ The software on the network server that controls the flow of e-mail.

Mailbox ▶ Where incoming e-mail messages are stored on a host or network server.

Mainframes ▶ Large, fast, and fairly expensive computers, generally used by business or government to provide centralized storage, processing, and management for large amounts of data and to provide that data on demand to many users.

Memory ▶ Electronic circuitry in a computer that holds data and program instructions waiting to be processed.

Menu ▶ A list of commands or options.

Menu bar ▶ Displays the menu titles.

Menu hierarchy ▶ Menus arranged in a hierarchical structure.

Menu item ▶ (also Menu option) A command listed on each line of the menu.

Menu option ▶ (also Menu item) A command listed on each line of the menu.

Microcomputers ▶ Also known as personal computers or PCs. The computers you typically find in homes and small businesses.

Millisecond ▶ A thousandth of a second. Used to measure access time.

Minicomputers ▶ Somewhat larger than microcomputers, generally used in business and industry for specific tasks, such as processing payroll.

Modem ▶ Transfers data from one computer to another over telephone lines.

Modifier keys ▶ The [Alt], [Ctrl] and [Shift] keys on the keyboard. Used in conjunction with other keys to issue commands.

Monitor ▶ A display device that converts the electrical signals from the computer into points of colored light on the screen to form an image.

Mouse ▶ A pointing device used to input data.

Multimedia ▶ An integrated collections of computer-based text, graphics, sound, animation, photo images, and video.

Network printer ▶ A printer that provides output capabilities to all the network users.

Network resources ▶ Devices shared by network users such as application software, storage space for data files, and printers other than those on your local workstation.

Network server ▶ A computer connected to the network that "serves," or distributes resources to network users.

Node ▶ Each device on a network, including workstations, servers, and printers.

Num Lock key ▶ A toggle key that switches between number keys and cursor keys on the numeric keypad.

Numeric keypad ▶ A calculator-style input device for numbers and arithmetic symbols.

On-line help ▶ Reference information frequently available within an application, accessible from a Help menu or by typing "HELP" at a command-line prompt.

On-line information ▶ Information obtained over the information highway.

On-line service ▶ A service that provides access to computer-based information and services for a fee. Also called a commercial information service.

Opening a file ▶ The process of retrieving data.

Operating system ▶ The software that controls the computer's use of its hardware resources such as memory and disk storage space.

Output ▶ The result produced by a computer

Output device ▶ A peripheral device that displays, prints, or transfers the results of processing from the computer memory.

Page Up ▶ Displays the previous screen of information.

Page Down ▶ Displays the next screen of information.

Pause key ▶ Stops the current task your computer is performing.

PC-compatibles ▶ Also referred to as IBM-compatibles. Computers based on the architecture of the first IBM microcomputer.

Peripheral device ▶ Equipment outside of or in addition to the computer, used with the computer. For example, the keyboard and the printer.

Physical storage ▶ How data is actually stored on the physical disk.

Pixels ▶ A matrix of small dots which form the display on a computer screen.

Platforms ► Microcomputer designs.

Plotter ► Uses pens to draw an image on paper.

Pointer ► Usually shaped like an arrow, the pointer moves on the screen in a way that corresponds to how you move the mouse on a hard surface like your desk.

Print Screen key ► Prints the contents of the screen when you use certain types of software. Other types of software the Print Screen key stores a copy of your screen in memory that you can manipulate or print with draw or paint software.

Priority mail ► A feature offered by some electronic mail systems which immediately alerts the recipient that an important e-mail message has arrived.

Process ► A systematic series of actions a computer uses to manipulate data.

Prompt ► A message displayed by the computer that asks for input from the user.

Promted dialog ► A user interface formed by a sequence of prompts.

Reading data ► The process of retrieving data.

Resolution ► A way of judging the sharpness of a display on a computer screen. The more dots your screen displays in the matrix, the higher the resolution.

Return receipt ► A feature offered by some electronic mail systems which sends a message back to you when a recipient receives your message.

Scanner ► Converts text or images on paper documents into an electronic format that the computer can display, print, and store.

Scroll Lock key ► The function of this key depends on the software you are using.

Shift key ► This key capitalizes letters and produces the top symbol on the keys that contain two symbols.

Sites ► The "towns" on the information highway. Computers of all descriptions—micros, minis, and mainframes.

Software ► Instructions and associated data, stored in electronic format, that direct the computer to accomplish a task.

Sound card ► A device installed inside a computer to give it capability to accept audio input from a microphone, play sound files stored on disks or CD-ROMs, and produce audio output through speakers or earphones.

Source file ► A file that contains instructions that a computer user can understand and that must be translated before a computer can execute them.

Stand-alone computer ► A computer that is not connected to a network.

Storage ► The area where data can be left on a permanent basis while it is not needed for processing.

Storage capacity ► The maximum amount of data that can be stored on a storage medium. Usually measured in kilobytes, megabytes, or gigabytes.

Storage device ► The mechanical apparatus that records and retrieves the data from the storage medium, such as a disk drive.

Storage medium ► The disk, tape, paper, or other substance that contains data. *Storage media* is the plural.

Storage technology ► A term that refers to a storage device and the media it uses.

Store and forward technology ► The ability to store information, such as an e-mail message for retrieval at a later time by a person other than the sender or person who stored the message.

Supercomputers ► The largest, fastest, and most expensive type of computer.

Support line ► A service offered over the phone by a hardware manufacturer or software publisher to customers who have questions about how to use a software or hardware product.

Syntax ► Specifies the sequence and punctuation for command words, parameters, and switches.

Syntax error ► A message conveyed by a computer if you misspell a command word, leave out required punctuation, or type the command words out of order.

System software ► Software that helps the computer carry out its basic operating tasks.

Taskbar ► Contains buttons that show you which software programs you are using.

Terminal ► A device used for input and output, but not for processing. If you are using a minicomputer system, you use a to input your processing requests and view the results.

Terminal ► A workstation on a host-terminal network. Has a keyboard and a screen, but does not have a local storage device, and does little or no processing on its own.

Toggle key ► A key that switches back and forth between two modes.

Tool bars ► Display buttons or tools that provide shortcuts to the commands on the menus.

Trackball ► A pointing device that has a rolling ball and unlike a mouse, doesn't move on the desk and therefore requires less space.

Tutorial ► A guided, step-by-step learning experience.

Uniform resource locator (URL) ► Each web page's unique address.

User ID ► A unique set of letters and numbers that serve as your "call sign" or "identification." The first part of an internet address. For example, "president" in the address *president@whitehouse.gov.*

User interface ► The means by which humans and computers communicate.

Vaporware ► Products that are announced but never made or marketed.

Web browser ► Software that facilitates access to the internet.

Web page ► Each image, video, or document stored as a file on the host computer that is accessed through the Internet and World Wide Web.

Wide area network (WAN) ► A network that covers a large geographical area.

Window ► Work areas similar to having different documents open at your desk. You can switch between different windows on the computer screen to work on different tasks.

Wizard ► A sequence of screens that direct you through multi-step software tasks such as creating a graph, a list of business contacts, or a fax cover sheet.

Workstation ► What your computer becomes when you physically connect your computer to a local area network, using a cable or other communications channel.

World Wide Web (WWW) ► A service on the Internet that currently offers some of the best organized and most accessible information.

Writing data ► The process of storing data.

Index